AF599537

UPON YOU

MY FELLOW SERVANTS

Upon You

My Fellow Servants

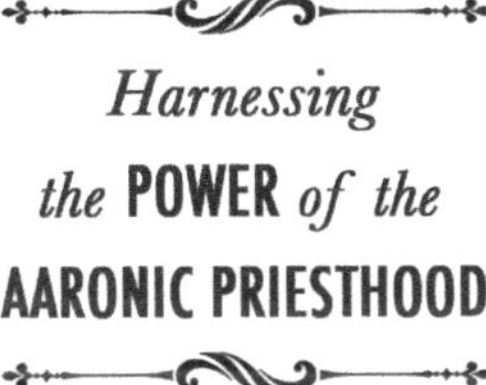

Harnessing the **POWER** *of the* **AARONIC PRIESTHOOD**

Nathan K. Nelson

CFI

An imprint of Cedar Fort, Inc.
Springville, Utah

© 2020 Nathan K. Nelson
All rights reserved.

No part of this book may be reproduced in any form whatsoever, whether by graphic, visual, electronic, film, microfilm, tape recording, or any other means, without prior written permission of the publisher, except in the case of brief passages embodied in critical reviews and articles.

This is not an official publication of The Church of Jesus Christ of Latter-day Saints. The opinions and views expressed herein belong solely to the author and do not necessarily represent the opinions or views of Cedar Fort, Inc. Permission for the use of sources, graphics, and photos is also solely the responsibility of the author.

ISBN 13: 978-1-4621-3784-8

Published by CFI, an imprint of Cedar Fort, Inc.
2373 W. 700 S., Springville, UT, 84663
Distributed by Cedar Fort, Inc., www.cedarfort.com

Library of Congress Control Number: 2020937949

Cover design by Wesley Wheeler
Cover design © 2020 Cedar Fort, Inc.

Printed in the United States of America

10 9 8 7 6 5 4 3 2 1

Printed on acid-free paper

For Amelia, Laura, Josh, and Megan

and

for Kara

May you be empowered with priesthood purpose
to prepare you for the coming of the Lord.

CONTENTS

Introduction 1

PART I: THE DEWS FROM HEAVEN 5

Chapter 1: The Power of Godliness 7
Chapter 2: A Preparatory Priesthood 15
Chapter 3: Parenting Priesthood Potential 29
Chapter 4: Keys of the Preparatory Priesthood 39
Chapter 5: The Gospel of Repentance and Baptism 57
Chapter 6: Preparing for Melchizedek Priesthood Power 71
Chapter 7: Fulfilling Your Duty to God 85
Chapter 8: Building on Pillars of Priesthood Power 97
Chapter 9: Sons and Daughters of Heavenly Parents 111

PART II: TO MY GREAT JOY 125

A Pattern of Love 129
A Pattern of Successful Service 135
A Pattern to Magnify Parents 145
A Pattern of Providing Provisions to Partake of the Atonement 151
A Pattern of Courage to Create Confidence 163

Conclusion 173
About the Author 175

INTRODUCTION

Upon you my fellow servants, in the name of Messiah, I confer upon you the priesthood of Aaron, which contains the keys of the gospel of repentance and of baptism, and the ministry of angels.

—DOCTRINE AND COVENANTS 13:1

The words above that recorded the events that occurred on May 15, 1829, should thrill every son and daughter of God. When I contemplate the reality that an angel from heaven, even the resurrected John the Baptist, would part the veil to visit a young prophet and his faithful companion, I am nothing short of overwhelmed.

Angels have long been an important component of God's communication to his prophets. The scriptures are replete with heavenly visitors. But what about today? We know Joseph Smith was visited by Moroni, Peter, James, John, and also John the Baptist, the latter of whom declared the keys to the ministry of angels to be restored. However, since those opening scenes in Church history, what is the role of angels in the continually unfolding restoration of the gospel of Jesus Christ?

This question concerning angels and their role in the gospel today has weighed on me for some time. As I stewed on this question, my thoughts were led to the familiar language in John the Baptist's conferral of the Aaronic Priesthood: "Upon you my fellow servants, in the name of Messiah, I confer upon you the priesthood of Aaron, which contains the keys to the gospel of repentance, and of baptism, and of the ministry of angels"

(D&C 13:1). I felt strongly that somewhere in those words were the answers to my questions.

Little did I know that a simple gospel question could result in an experience as rich as the one I have had over the four years spent writing a book about the power and authority of the Aaronic Priesthood. Without a doubt, the ministry of angels is a living reality in our day, and the Aaronic Priesthood has a living and active purpose in the restored gospel plan to prepare people for the coming of the Savior, Jesus Christ.

I have directed my thoughts in this book largely to the young men ordained to offices within the Aaronic Priesthood. However, I have sought to provide enough evidence to warrant the interest of parents, leaders, and young women to discover their own unique purposes to harness Aaronic Priesthood power. No matter who you are, I hope that you will gain new insights on the Aaronic Priesthood and that you will develop a renewed commitment to obtain your own personal revelation for how you can contribute to the Lord's preparatory priesthood.

For my own understanding, where possible, I have sought to apply the teaching methods outlined in Doctrine and Covenants 88:78 where the Lord provides this formula for learning: "That you may be instructed more perfectly in theory, in principle, in doctrine."

This book consists of two separate parts. Part I is a series of chapters that seek to account for the revealed doctrine surrounding the Aaronic Priesthood and the impact of those truths on Aaronic Priesthood holders. Part I leans on the Young Men's theme for a framework to promote an understanding of Aaronic Priesthood doctrines. In doing so, Part I also focuses on the personal development and testimony that the Lord requires of His Aaronic Priesthood holders.

At the end of each chapter in Part I is a short section that will invite you to further explore (individually or with your family or quorum) the doctrines, principles, and theories of the topics introduced in the chapter. I have benefited from this pattern of gospel learning by dividing my efforts to learn and obtain revelation into three categories:

1. Doctrine—Seek to understand the *why*.
2. Principle—Seek to understand the *what*.
3. Theory—Seek to understand the *how*.

Perhaps you are already familiar with this pattern. I am confident that if you will take the time to accept the invitations at the end of each chapter you too will obtain specific direction that will help you become more faithful and effective as you sustain the Aaronic Priesthood.

In my own pursuit of understanding the doctrines around the ministry of angels and the priesthood of Aaron, I have found many of the "theories" or the "how's" to be well demonstrated by one of the stars of the Book of Mormon—Helaman. As the captain of the famed stripling warriors, Helaman proved to be the ultimate Aaronic Priesthood leader.

Part II of this book leans on Helaman's experience as a leader and inspirer of young men. It is written with the Aaronic Priesthood holder in mind but focuses more on the leadership aspects of Aaronic Priesthood service. The leadership patterns identified can be applied by quorum presidencies, advisers, and parents. They are simple but effective patterns that can bless you as an Aaronic Priesthood holder no matter if you are a seasoned quorum president, bishop, or even the newest ordained deacon.

Above all, as you read and explore the doctrines, principles, and theories associated with the Aaronic Priesthood, I hope you will gain a sense of identity that you are on the Lord's team and that He knows you. I hope you will gain a sense of personal priesthood purpose in recognizing the specific role of the Aaronic Priesthood within the gospel of Jesus Christ. I am confident that as you step forward and elevate your commitment to your purpose as an Aaronic Priesthood holder, you will strengthen your relationship with the Savior, and the days will come when you will see God in your priesthood service.

PART I

The Dews from Heaven

And the doctrine of the priesthood shall distill upon thy soul as the dews from heaven.

—DOCTRINE AND COVENANTS 121:45

CHAPTER 1

The Power of Godliness

I Am a Beloved Son of God

Therefore, in the ordinances thereof, the power of godliness is manifest. And without the ordinances thereof, and the authority of the priesthood, the power of godliness is not manifest unto men in the flesh.

—DOCTRINE AND COVENANTS 84:20–21

On a stormy night in 1752, Benjamin Franklin ventured out from the safety of his home in Philadelphia equipped with a kite, a small metal key, and a question. Could the electric fire that erupted from the sky on nights such as this be harnessed? Were there fundamental elements invisible to the eye that could provide new understanding of this power that seemed to only belong to the gods of ancient times? Could he prove that there was, in fact, an electrical energy consisting of positive and negative particles that might one day be bridled for the benefit of all mankind?

Though he had been mocked for his hypothesis, with undaunted optimism he built his kite and launched it into the windy air. With enthusiasm he described his experiment and the effects of the negative charged energy on his kite, the key, and the twine that secured them together before trickling down to a small glass jar that included a crude capacitor that carried the hope of serving as a collector for the heavenly power:

> To the End of the Twine, next the Hand, is to be tied a silk Ribbon, and where the Twine and the silk join, a Key may be fastened. This Kite is to be raised when a Thunder Gust appears to be coming on, and the Person who holds the String must stand within a Door, or Window, or under some Cover, so that the Silk Ribbon may not be wet; and Care must be taken that the Twine does not touch the Frame of the Door or Window. As soon as any of the Thunder Clouds come over the Kite, the pointed Wire will draw the Electric Fire from them, and the Kite, with all the Twine, will be electrified, and the loose Filaments of the Twine will stand out every Way, and be attracted by an approaching Finger. And when the Rain has wet the Kite and Twine, so that it can conduct the Electric Fire freely, you will find it stream out plentifully from the Key on the Approach of your Knuckle.[1]

I like to imagine Franklin's excitement as electricity literally filled the air and caused the threads in the twine to stand on end. Franklin's key unlocked the gate for other inspired individuals who each made tremendous contributions of their own to find purpose for this eternal power. Electricity would, in time, be harnessed to become a source of great power, giving light and enabling knowledge to be shared throughout the earth.

The key to applying this power for the benefit of man was to define the laws and establish the elements that measure the magnitude of this force. Soon a new vernacular, or language, was established that included words such as *amps*, *ohms*, *volts*, and *watts*. Amps would measure the speed of electricity running through a circuit. Like water pressure in a hose, volts would serve to measure the pressure of the electricity within a circuit. An ohm became the defining measurement of the amount of resistance placed on an electrical force. Finally, watts would become the very familiar term to define the absolute power produced by an electrical circuit.

Just sixty-eight years following Franklin's experiment, a young man similarly left his home with an honest inquiry occupying his mind and heart. Like Franklin's revelation on electricity, on that beautiful and sacred spring morning, the young prophet-to-be would make a discovery of even greater magnitude as he similarly set his eyes toward the heavens. In time, he too would learn a new set of laws and means for measuring this power of a loving God that was being restored to the earth for the benefit of His children.

Like lightning in Franklin's bottle, young Joseph soon learned of the immensity and majesty of God's power. When Joseph entered the grove in the spring of 1820, he took with him the specific question of which church he should join. In addition to answering Joseph's specific question, in a very clear, but understated way, the Savior announced the restoration of the laws and ordinances of His gospel and declared to the world that all of God's children would now be able to fully partake of the Atonement to find peace, hope, and reconciliation with their Father in Heaven through the re-establishment of His priesthood power.

Consider the words of the Savior to Joseph on that marvelous morning and look for what the Lord tells Joseph about the words *godliness* and *power*: "I was answered that I must join none of them, for they were all wrong; and the Personage who addressed me said that all their creeds were an abomination in his sight; that those professors were all corrupt; that: '*they draw near to me with their lips, but their hearts are far from me,* ***they teach for doctrines the commandments of men, having a form of godliness, but they deny the power thereof***'" (Joseph Smith—History 2:19; emphasis added).

Those final words of the Savior give tremendous insight into the integral role the priesthood would play in the restoration of His gospel. Regarding the other sects and beliefs of the day, the Savior stated that they "teach for doctrines the commandments of men, having a form of godliness, but they deny the power thereof." The words *godliness* and *power* provide an interesting insight into what happened on that spring morning.

What is godliness, and what is this power that enables it? To be like God is the fulfillment of women and men's greatest potential. Before coming to earth, each of us lived in the presence of God, and there we desired to be like our loving Father in Heaven. Through his glorious plan of salvation, our Father prepared a way that we might reach our full potential as His spirit children to progress and become as He is.

Just as a child grows to embody the attributes of his or her parents, our purpose here on Earth is to grow and progress to become like our Father in Heaven. We know and trust that He is perfect and that He enjoys eternal happiness. Because of that, we want to grow and progress to similarly embody His attributes and character.

Critical to the fulfillment of His plan and our eternal purpose is the need to overcome the otherwise permanent effects of mortality, specifically death and sin, to become like our Father who lives free from both of these impediments. The power required to enable this progression and development is only available to God's children as they become unified with Him through the Atonement of His Son, Jesus Christ. Ultimately this change is effectuated as we make covenants and receive saving ordinances that are facilitated only by the power of God through priesthood power.

When Heavenly Father took His beloved Son to the grove, He knew very well that the world lacked the fulness of this power of godliness, this power to become as He is. With the Father and Son's arrival, Their identity and attributes would no longer have to be a mystery to mankind, and the reality that we are all His children divinely endowed to become like Him was suddenly obvious.

Twelve years after the First Vision, the Lord would shed further light on this power and the potential for godliness that He referenced in the grove in what is now known as the revelation on the priesthood. The Lord explained to Joseph that it is in the *ordinances* administered by God's priesthood that the *power of godliness*, or the power to partake of the Atonement to become like our Heavenly Father, is made manifest to His children on Earth.

As you read the following verses, look for ways the Lord references both the Aaronic and greater priesthoods. Also look for what the Lord says about where we can see His power being made manifest to us.

> And the Lord confirmed a priesthood also upon Aaron and his seed, throughout all their generations, which priesthood also continueth and abideth forever with the priesthood which is after the holiest order of God.

> And this greater priesthood administereth the gospel and holdeth the key of the mysteries of the kingdom, even the key of the knowledge of God. Therefore, in the ordinances thereof the power of godliness is manifest.
>
> And without the ordinances thereof, and the authority of the priesthood, the power of godliness is not manifest unto men in the flesh. (D&C 84:18–21)

Did you see it? The Lord references both priesthoods and then says that it is in the ordinances where the power to become like Him, the power of godliness, is manifest. Think about what this means for you. What ordinances have you received? What ordinances have you participated in? How have you seen those ordinances enable your or others to become more like God?

As I reflect on this verse, I am reminded of what the Lord told Joseph in the grove about what was absent from the earth: "They teach for doctrines, the commandments of men, having a form of godliness, but denying the power thereof" (JS—H 1:19). Throughout the Apostasy, men identified what they perceived to be commandments to perform ordinances as they understood them to be outlined in scripture. As people throughout history administered various forms of baptisms and sacraments within different religious traditions, they identified a way to pursue the Atonement. But they had, as the Savior stated, only a form of godliness. Without the restoration of priesthood power, these ordinances relied only on the merits of men's understanding and consequently denied the power of God's true influence or His godliness that is manifest only through ordinances performed under authorized priesthood power.

It is interesting to observe that the Lord's first statement in the grove was a reference to the need for a restoration of priesthood power and its associated ordinances. The Lord declared that the power to overcome the frailties of mortality and to become like God is found in the ordinances administered under the restored priesthood power.

Like the people who came after Franklin and blessed the world through their diligent efforts to understand the laws and define the elements of electrical power, we, as members of Christ's restored church, have a similar solemn opportunity and responsibility to enable the establishment of priesthood power to bring light, knowledge, hope, and happiness to all of God's children. Like the prophet Joseph, we too have an obligation to allow the doctrine of the priesthood to distill upon our souls as the dews from heaven.

Establishing God's power on earth begins with the preparatory priesthood. The dews from heaven will distill doctrine as we seek to be taught by the Holy Ghost, who can prompt thoughts that enlighten and remind us of our understanding of the power and potential of the Aaronic Priesthood. Through this powerful priesthood process, we can experience a renewed joy in understanding what it means to possess the keys of the gospel of repentance, baptism, and the ministry of angels. Furthermore, we can look to the beloved Aaronic Priesthood holders in our lives and be filled with desire to help them realize their priesthood potential.

As stewards of the Aaronic priesthood, we should be inspired to find ways to maximize the volts that measure priesthood pressure, or perhaps more eloquently stated, priesthood influence on the world. We need to be prompted with ideas to increase the amps of the speed and efficiency of the Aaronic Priesthood quorums that we sustain and to which we pertain. In understanding the magnitude of Aaronic Priesthood potential, we should do everything we can to increase the ohms of resistance to the evil that seeks to derail Aaronic Priesthood purposes. Finally, as we harness this heavenly power, we can experience the watts that measure the true power of godliness being established in our families, wards, and throughout the world by virtue of the Aaronic Priesthood and its purpose to prepare each of us for the coming of the Lord.

NOTE

1. Letter from Benjamin Franklin to Peter Collison, October 19, 1752. See I. Bernard Cohen's *Benjamin Franklin's Science* (Cambridge, MA: Harvard University Press, 1996), 66.

THE POWER OF GODLINESS

I Am a Beloved Son of God

DOCTRINE

Read Joseph Smith—History 1:19.

Look for Jesus Christ to acknowledge to Joseph Smith the absence of priesthood authority with words such as *godliness* and *power.*

Read Doctrine and Covenants 84:18–21.

Look for the Savior to teach the importance of priesthood ordinances as the means for pursuing godliness.

PRINCIPLE

Lead your quorum or family in a discussion.

- What is the relationship between pursuing godliness and priesthood power?
- How have the events of the Restoration influenced your understanding of your divine nature as a son or daughter of a Heavenly Father?

THEORY

Journal your thoughts on the following questions:

- In what ways have you experienced high voltage priesthood influence to inspire you in your own personal decisions to come unto Christ?
- What does it mean to you to increase the amps or speed and efficiency of priesthood power?
- In what ways have you experienced the ohms of resistance to evil because of your association with priesthood power?
- How has priesthood power prepared you and your family to meet the Savior?

CHAPTER 2

A Preparatory Priesthood

He Has a Work for Me to Do

To make ready a people prepared for the Lord.

—LUKE 1:17

The summer of 1999 was a challenging one for me as a missionary in Salvador, Brazil. I had just turned twenty years old and felt sorry for myself during some lonely days. I wallowed in the fact that my family back home would never know the twenty-year-old me, given that I would pass that entire year away from them.

I had just been made a senior companion to a new missionary fresh from the Missionary Training Center. About this time, my companion and I met a man named Fernando who owned a small newspaper stand near our house. Fernando was a blessing from the Lord. He was always easy to find because he was only ever in one of two places—his newspaper stand or in his house, which happened to be just a few steps away. Fernando did not venture far because he was completely blind and had been from the time he was a small child.

Fernando easily accepted our invitation to hear our message. In fact, he accepted just about everything we taught him. I will always remember the sweet experience it was visiting him every day to read aloud to him from the Book of Mormon. As we read and shared testimony, Fernando simply accepted everything without reservation.

However, as we began discussing baptism with him, it was not him, but rather I, who began to have real doubts about his commitment. Teaching him had been almost too easy. Throughout our time together, he never had a significant question or even a doubt; he just said "yes." In a way it was awesome, and yet, because it had been so easy, I continued to have serious questions about whether we really should encourage him to move so quickly to baptism. I questioned whether he would stay active and how he would get to church, especially with his visual impairment, in a city where few members owned cars and most rode the bus.

Reluctantly, I called our zone leader and invited him to interview Fernando for baptism. Of course, the interview went swimmingly, and the day came that we picked Fernando up and took him with us to the church where we had a tender baptismal service. I was happy for him and yet struggled to know if my work was really the work that the Lord had wanted done or whether I had just committed this man to a covenant that he would struggle to keep. Just a few days following his baptism, my concerns were compounded when I learned that Fernando's girlfriend was expecting a baby.

I was soon transferred and for years wondered what had happened to Fernando. I lacked the faith to believe that he had the ability to stay active because of his circumstances. I allowed my doubts to impede my faith. My time in the area had been short, and I did not do a good job of staying in touch with Fernando. Nearly twenty years passed, during which I had an occasional nagging to know what happened to my friend in Salvador, the city named for the Savior.

In the spring of 2018, I had an opportunity to return to this city that had shaped so much of me. I was able to meet up with a friend in the area who I had also taught and who had been assigned to minister to Fernando for several years. I confessed that I had long wondered what happened to my blind friend. I soon learned that Fernando was very active in the Church and had been to the temple. Beyond thrilled to hear this news, I asked if we could pay him a visit.

We walked hurriedly to that very same house with the newspaper stand still out front and knocked on Fernando's front door. Fernando came to his balcony and invited us up. When we met, tears filled both of our eyes as we embraced. I had been right in that he had not gone far in the twenty years that had passed, but I had also been very wrong to doubt the Lord's hand in his life. As we stood there smiling and celebrating this tender mercy of the Lord to be together again, Fernando exclaimed, "All these years I have dreamt that someday when I get to the other side of the veil, I would have the opportunity to see the missionaries who brought me the gospel, and here you are, in my home again!" I cannot describe the joy I felt to stand as a witness to the work of the Good Shepherd who numbers every one of his sheep.

As if this was not enough, I soon met a young man living with Fernando, who I quickly learned was his eighteen-year-old son. The same boy who was just newly in the womb at the time of Fernando's baptism was now a priest in the Aaronic Priesthood preparing to serve a mission of his own. I was overjoyed at the opportunity I had to repent for doubting the Lord. The work that I had done as a young missionary was never my work. As a beloved son of God, I knew clearly that this was *His* work that I had been called to do.

You are beloved sons of God called and ordained into this great preparatory priesthood, and He similarly has a work for you to do. As Aaronic Priesthood holders, you are in the midst of a great preparation for the life that you will each create for yourselves. Filled with enthusiasm, you are preparing for missions, careers, families, adventures, and all that awaits you. It may, therefore, be seemingly obvious why we refer to the priesthood you hold as the preparatory priesthood as you prepare for the work and opportunities that the Lord has for you to do.

Is this, then, really why we call it the preparatory priesthood? Is it because the Aaronic priesthood is given to you during this preparatory phase of your life? Is it referred to as preparatory only because of the ways that it prepares a young man for the greater priesthood that is still to come? What is this preparatory work that you are called to do?

To learn more about the preparatory purposes of the Aaronic Priesthood, we can look to the man who was sent to restore the Aaronic Priesthood to Joseph Smith—John the Baptist. You will remember the famous picture of Joseph and Oliver kneeling in the woods while the resurrected angel, John the Baptist, stands over the two men with hands placed on Joseph's head, conferring upon him the Aaronic Priesthood.

To capture the magnitude of this moment, we have to remind ourselves that this heavenly messenger is the same John who baptized Jesus and who was born with the sacred mission of preparing the way for Jesus Christ. John the Baptist was, in fact, the Great Preparer. It was he whose life fulfilled and exemplified the divinely appointed purposes of the preparatory priesthood.

As modern-day fellow servants who possess this same priesthood, we would do well to learn more about our friend John. You will certainly remember a few of the amazing details that surrounded his birth—about being born to parents who were just plain *old*. John the Baptist was a miracle baby, if there ever was one. In Luke 1 we can gain insights into the miracle of his life and the beautiful prophesies of his preparatory purposes.

You will remember the more notable events of John's birth. His father, Zacharias, was a priest who righteously served in the temple. While he and his wife, Sariah, were faithful servants, they were "stricken in years," and it seemed impossible that they would be blessed with children. Yet, on a sacred day as Zacharias performed his holy work to burn the incense at the altar of the temple, the faithful prophet to be was visited by an angel, known as Gabriel.

Speaking to Zacharias, the angel prophesied that he and his aged wife, Sariah, would soon become the parents of a baby boy. In this moment of heavenly awe, Zacharias would be struck dumb before being given this sacred prophecy regarding the boy who would be called the Baptist. He let his doubts overcome his faith, thus rendering him unable to speak. Imagine, though, being there in the dimly lit temple on that day and being with Zacharias as he was enveloped by the light and love of God's angel who spoke these words to the elderly servant of the Lord:

> For he shall be great in the sight of the Lord, and shall drink neither wine nor strong drink; and he shall be filled with the Holy Ghost, even from his mother's womb. And many of the children of Israel shall he turn to the Lord their God. "And he shall go before him in the spirit and power of Elias, to turn the hearts of the fathers to the children, and the disobedient to the wisdom of the just; *to make ready a people prepared for the Lord*" (Luke 1:15–17; emphasis added).

Unable to speak for nine months, Zacharias was compelled to ponder alone and keep secret the details of this sacred prophecy. Can you imagine what that was like for Zacharias and Sariah to not be able to effectively communicate their excitement for nine months? Zacharias would have to be pretty creative and convincing for what was likely one of the earliest gender reveals.

In those days, friends and family would gather at the temple on the eighth day following a baby's birth for the baby's naming and circumcision. As people gathered on that eighth day following John's miraculous birth, with Zacharias still unable to speak, there must have been great anticipation with none greater than what was had by Zacharias himself. The temple priests began by following custom and announced to those who were gathered that the babe would be given the name of Zacharias, after his father.

However, before the temple priests could proceed with the naming rites and in a powerful example of a woman's capacity to sustain and strengthen the Lord's priesthood authority, Elisabeth immediately stepped forward and declared that the boy's name would not be Zacharias, but John. Bewildered, the priests looked to the muted father who confirmed Elisabeth's declaration by humbly scrawling the Hebrew equivalent of J-O-H-N onto a writing tablet.

Having exercised their faith to break with the custom and follow the angel's commandment to name the boy John, Zacharias's tongue was finally loosed. In this sacred and unbridled moment, Zacharias offered powerful perspective on the potential within the preparatory priesthood that his newborn son would soon possess. Immediately he was compelled to testify of the Savior and His restorative role.

As you read these words of Zacharias, look for how he testifies of Jesus Christ. Look for Zacharias to explain how he understands

Christ's purpose to "perform the mercy promised to our fathers and to remember the covenant." He knew that this Jesus who would soon be born was truly the Redeemer of Israel. Finally, notice that before sharing the angel's prophecy about the baby John, Zacharias first bore an exuberant testimony of the Savior. Here are his words:

> Blessed be the Lord God of Israel; for he hath visited and redeemed his people, And hath raised up an horn of salvation for us in the house of his servant David; As he spake by the mouth of his holy prophets, which have been since the world began: That we should be saved from our enemies and from the hand of all that hate us; To perform the mercy promised to our fathers and to remember his holy covenant; The truth which he sware to our father Abraham, That he would grant unto us, that we being delivered out of the hand of our enemies might serve him without fear, In holiness and righteousness before him, all the days of our life. (Luke 1:68–75)

Following his beautiful testimony of the divinely appointed role of the Master who was soon to arrive, Zacharias turned his attention to his own son and echoed the earlier words of the angel by prophesying of John's preparatory role. Look for the word *prepare* and pay attention to how it applies to John's prophesied priesthood service.

> And thou, child, shalt be called the prophet of the Highest: for thou shalt *go before the face of the Lord to prepare his ways*; To give knowledge of salvation unto his people by the remission of their sins, Through the tender mercy of our God; whereby the dayspring from on high hath visited us, To give light to them that sit in darkness and in the shadow of death, to guide our feet into the way of peace. (Luke 1:76–79; emphasis added)

Did you see it? Did you see John's Aaronic Priesthood purpose? His purpose was simply but clearly to "go before the face of the Lord to prepare his ways." This simple statement gives purpose not only for John but also for all Aaronic Priesthood holders.

Think about this statement and break it down with me. To go before the Lord is to go ahead of Him. Before Jesus can come, John (and you) will go first. Why? To prepare His ways. "To give light to them that sit in darkness" and to "guide the feet" of those who follow "into the way of peace."

This declaration, along with the earlier prophecy given by the angel Gabriel, announced to the world not only the specific role of John the Baptist but also articulated the full purposes of the Aaronic Priesthood that John was foreordained to embody and accomplish both anciently and in modern times.

In examining both Gabriel and Zacharias's prophecies, we can identify that core to John's identity as the preeminent Aaronic Priesthood holder are the overarching priesthood purposes that he was foreordained to accomplish—both individually and as the forerunner for deacons, teachers, priests, and bishops to look to as they work to harness the full power of the Aaronic Priesthood.

In reviewing this divine mandate announced by both Gabriel and Zacharias in the first chapter of Luke to "go *before* the Lord," we can identify at least six Aaronic Priesthood purposes that can lift our understanding of what it means to possess the preparatory priesthood:

1. Turn the hearts of the fathers to the children (verse 17).
2. Turn the disobedient to the wisdom of the just (verse 17).
3. To make ready a people prepared for the coming of the Lord and to go before His Face and prepare His ways (verses 17 and 76).
4. Give knowledge of salvation unto his people by the remission of their sins (verse 77).
5. Give light to them that sit in darkness and in the shadow of death (verse 79).
6. Guide our feet into the way of peace (verse 79).

These priesthood purposes given to John millennia ago are eternal and are profoundly evident in Aaronic Priesthood service today. As you ponder their application, you will find renewed purpose in your priesthood service that prepares both you and others for the coming of the Lord. Here are just a few examples of how these Aaronic Priesthood purposes are evident today.

Your time spent researching your family history and participating in temple ordinances is your personal fulfillment of the prophecy "to turn the hearts of the fathers to the children" (Luke 1:17).

As you participate in the saving ordinances of baptism and the sacrament, are you not in a very real way turning "the disobedient to the wisdom of the just" (Luke 1:17) and giving "light to them that sit in darkness?" (Luke 1:79).

As you fulfill ministering assignments, prepare spiritual messages, and extend invitations to others to come unto Christ, in various ways you are fulfilling the prophecies of the preparatory priesthood to "prepare his ways" and to "give knowledge of salvation" and to "guide their feet into the way of peace." Through what you may often view as simple service, you are truly "making ready a people prepared for the coming of the Lord."

Think about what Gabriel said about John—that he would "go before the Lord." What could it mean to "go before"? Obviously, John was born before Jesus. We also know that he preached the gospel to the people before Jesus began His ministry. The angel Gabriel used an interesting phrase to describe this mission to "go before." He described John's role as the Elias, saying, "He shall go before him in the spirit and power of Elias" (Luke 1:17).

What is an Elias, you ask? Elias is a title given in ancient times to prophets and people of prominence who were forerunners, or in other words, people who came before something or someone of even greater significance. In this case, John is the Elias who came before the Savior to prepare the way for His gospel to be established. He also serves as an Elias for Aaronic Priesthood holders today by setting the standard for their service.

John the Baptist's title of Elias, or forerunner, is made clear in several verses in the New Testament. As you read these, look to learn how John served as an Elias who prepared the way for Jesus Christ.

> And if eye will receive it, verily, he (John) was the Elias, who was for to come and *prepare all things*. (JST, Matthew 11:15; emphasis added)

> Among them that are born of women there hath not risen a greater than John the Baptist. (Matthew 11:11)

> But I say unto you, Who is Elias? Behold, *this is Elias, whom I send to prepare the way before me.* Then the disciples understood that he spake unto them of John the Baptist. (JST, Matthew 17:10–14; emphasis added)

Heavenly Father selected one of His greatest to be the Elias for Jesus Christ. There is one last verse that is particularly interesting because John both acknowledges that while he is the Elias of the *preparation*, he is not the Elias of the *restoration*. In this verse John explains the difference between his preparatory purpose and the full purpose of Christ's ministry. The Bible Dictionary articulates further that "these passages are sufficiently clarified to show that anciently two Eliases were spoken of, one as a *preparer* and the other a *restorer.* John was sent to prepare the way before Jesus, Jesus Himself being the Restorer who brought back the gospel and the Melchizedek Priesthood to the Jews in His day. In this particular instance, there is reflected also the comparative functions of the Aaronic and Melchizedek Priesthoods."

> And he [John] confessed, and denied not that he was Elias; but confessed, saying; I am not the Christ. And they asked him, saying; How then art thou Elias? And he said, *I am not that Elias who was to restore all things.* And they asked him saying, art thou that prophet? And he answered, No. Then said they unto him, Who art thou? That we may give an answer to them that sent us. What sayest thou of thyself? He said, I am the voice of one crying in the wilderness, *Make straight the way of the Lord,* as saith the prophet Esaias. And they who were sent were of the Pharisees. And they asked him, and said unto him; Why baptizest thou then, if thou be not the Christ, nor Elias who was to restore all things, neither that prophet? John answered them, saying; I baptize with water, but there standeth one among you who ye know not; He it is of whom I bear record. He is that prophet even Elias, who, coming after me, is preferred before me, whose shoe's latchet I am not worthy to unloose, or whose place I am not able to fill for he shall baptize not only with water but with fire, and with the Holy Ghost. (JST, John 1:21–28; emphasis added)

Understanding John the Baptist's role as a preparatory Elias tasked with preparing the way for the Lord to come unto His children is imperative for those who hold the authority to administer the keys of the Aaronic Priesthood in the Church of Jesus Christ today. Just like John the Baptist, in a very specific and sacred way, each of the familiar

Aaronic Priesthood offices today have a special role to serve as a preparatory Elias for the men, women, and children in their respective wards and branches. The keys of the Aaronic Priesthood underscore and obligate bishops, priests, teachers, and deacons to understand and fulfill their unique role to accomplish each of the priesthood purposes first identified by the angel Gabriel and thereafter by Zacharias to make ready a people prepared for the coming of the Lord. Having been divinely appointed to serve as the preparatory Elias to the Savior Himself, John would develop a perfect understanding of the conversion that occurs when an individual is well prepared and qualified to receive the invitation to come unto Christ.

Certainly, throughout his own mortal ministry, John would come to know very well the difference between, and even to judge, whether a person was well prepared to encounter and receive the Savior or not. His teaching and preparatory service enabled those of his day who would encounter the Lord to experience the healing, enabling, and redeeming power of His Atonement. Likely, he saw how even the Apostles changed or converted from being people prepared to meet the Savior to individuals who had prepared themselves to serve as special witnesses of Jesus Christ.

With this experience, John the Baptist had a clear vision of the need for people to be prepared to meet the Master. He was seasoned in utilizing the combined Aaronic Priesthood keys of the ministering of angels and the keys of the gospel of repentance to accomplish the Aaronic Priesthood purposes outlined to his father by the angel Gabriel.

As we see the power and influence that he had in preparing the way for the Lord to come to the people in his day, it becomes increasingly clear why it was John the Baptist who would come again in his role as Elias the Preparer. Now as a ministering angel to Joseph Smith and Oliver Cowdery, John came to restore the preparatory priesthood and deliver again those same ancient priesthood purposes so that in these great days of the Restoration, we, like John, may also be able to establish a people prepared for the coming of the Lord.

Some of the most beautiful language in all of scripture is tucked away at the end of the Pearl of Great Price in a font that nearly requires a magnifying glass to uncover its luster and value. On the final two pages of Joseph Smith—History, Oliver Cowdery eloquently describes what it was like to be at the side of the prophet as the restored gospel was unfolded before them. In a lengthy essay, he articulates both the implications and emotions associated with John the Baptist's visit to restore the Aaronic Priesthood. Pay attention to the sacred feelings that come to you as you read some of his words and contemplate the majesty of what he experienced:

> These were days never to be forgotten—to sit under the sound of a voice dictated by the inspiration of heaven, awakened the utmost gratitude of this bosom . . . and we only waited for the commandment to be given "Arise and be baptized."
>
> This was not long desired before it was realized. The Lord, who is rich in mercy and ever willing to answer the consistent prayer of the humble, after we had called upon Him in a fervent manner, aside from the abodes of men, condescended to manifest to us His will. On a sudden, as from the midst of eternity, the voice of the Redeemer spake peace to us, while the veil was parted and the angel of God came down clothed with glory, and delivered the anxiously looked for message, and the keys of the Gospel of repentance. *What joy! What wonder! What amazement! While the world was racked and distracted—while millions were groping as the blind for the wall, and while all men were resting upon uncertainty, as a general mass, our eyes beheld, our ears heard, as in the 'blaze of day'; yes more—above the glitter of the May sunbeam, which then shed its brilliancy over the face of nature! Then his voice though mild, pierced to the center, and his words, 'I am thy fellow-servant,' dispelled every fear. We listened, we gazed, we admired! 'Twas the voice of an angel from glory, 'twas a message from the Most High! And as we heard we rejoiced, while His love enkindled upon our souls, and we were wrapped in the vision of the Almighty! Where was room for doubt? Nowhere, uncertainty had fled, doubt had sunk no more to rise, while fiction and deception had fled forever!*
>
> But, dear brother, think, further think for a moment, what joy filled our hearts, and with what surprise we must have bowed, (for who would not have bowed the knee for such a blessing?) when we received under his hand the Holy Priesthood as he said, *"Upon you my fellow-servants, in the name of Messiah, I confer this Priesthood and this authority, which shall remain upon the earth, that the Sons of Levi may yet offer an offering unto the Lord in righteousness!"*
>
> I shall not attempt to paint to you the feelings of this heart, nor the majestic beauty and glory which surrounded us on this occasion;

> *but you will believe me when I say, that earth, nor men, with the eloquence of time, cannot begin to clothe the language in as interesting and sublime a manner as this holy personage.* No; nor has this earth power to give the joy, to bestow the peace, or comprehend the wisdom which was contained in each sentence as they were delivered by the power of the Holy Spirit!... The assurance that we were in the presence of an angel, the certainty that we heard the voice of Jesus, and the truth unsullied as it flowed from a pure personage, dictated by the will of God, is to me past description, and I shall ever look upon this expression of the Savior's goodness with wonder and thanksgiving while I am permitted to tarry; and in those mansions where perfection dwells and sin never comes, I hope to adore in that day which shall never cease. (Testimony of Oliver Cowdery, Joseph Smith—History; emphasis added)

In reading this lengthy and verbose text, one can feel Oliver's struggle to characterize the magnificence of these moments with the limited medium that was his pen. I love to feel the power, truth, and confirming testimony that are deeply seeded in Oliver's words.

These were days truly never to be forgotten. I like to contemplate the feelings of Zacharias that were silenced for those many months following his angelic visit and compare them with Oliver's language and emotions. Both had similar experiences in witnessing the majesty of the Lord as He delivered the keys that would unlock the power of His beautiful plan of happiness. Both men received not only a deep realization of the infinite power of the priesthood but also were given a clear understanding of its administrative purposes. Finally, both men were also given a mandate to distribute both the authority and power of the Aaronic Priesthood in order for the Lord to accomplish the purposes of His preparatory priesthood.

As we reflect on these two magnificent accounts of heavenly visitations, we would be remiss not to contemplate how well both the authority and power of the Aaronic Priesthood are experienced by those under its influence today. In so doing, we might pay attention to identify both the ways that we have witnessed the distribution of the *authority* of the Aaronic priesthood and the ways that we have witnessed the distribution of the *power* of the Aaronic Priesthood.

As the Church has grown in the nearly two centuries since the heavens were parted on that miraculous morning, prophets and apostles have provided guidance and counsel along with various programs and teachings to aid the distribution of the Lord's authority and power throughout the earth.

In a conference talk given in April 2010, President Boyd K. Packer called attention to the distribution of priesthood authority and priesthood power when he stated:

> We have done very well at distributing the authority of the priesthood. . . . But distributing the authority of the priesthood has raced, I think, ahead of distributing the power of the priesthood. The power of the Priesthood does not have the strength that it should have and will not have until the power of the priesthood is firmly fixed in the families as it should be.
>
> Authority in the priesthood comes by way of ordination; power in the priesthood comes through faithful and obedient living in honoring covenants. It is increased by exercising and using the priesthood in righteousness.[1]

The Lord needs a powerful preparatory priesthood to accomplish His purposes. His expectations are great, and His children have been given both the keys and the potential to fulfill His preparatory purposes. It is true that He has a work for you and me to do. As we study both ancient and modern revelations regarding the Aaronic Priesthood keys, we too can have John's and Oliver's perspectives to see clearly the need to leverage Aaronic Priesthood keys to stand tall in Aaronic Priesthood offices. By following the examples of John and Oliver, we can overcome the doubts that will inevitably afflict us as we are called to His work.

In obtaining a renewed and deeper understanding of the potential of the Aaronic Priesthood, we can celebrate our own days that are never to be forgotten. In so doing, we can qualify ourselves for our own moments of angelic ministry that we might ultimately find ourselves prepared to answer the call to deliver Aaronic Priesthood power and thus fulfill our duty to make ready a people prepared for the coming of the Lord.

NOTE

1. Boyd K. Packer, "The Power of the Priesthood," *Ensign*, May 2010, 9.

A PREPARATORY PRIESTHOOD

He Has a Work for Me to Do

DOCTRINE

Read Luke 1 and focus on the following verses: 15–17 (Gabriel's prophecy); 76–79 (Zacharias's prophecy).

Look for the promises of the preparatory priesthood given to John to help him prepare people for the ways of the Lord.

PRINCIPLE

Discuss with your family and quorum the following promises given to John and how they relate to your Aaronic Priesthood service today:

- Turn the hearts of the fathers to the children.
- Turn the disobedient to the wisdom of the just.
- Prepare His ways.
- Give knowledge of salvation unto his people by the remission of their sins.
- Give light to them that sit in darkness and in the shadow of death.
- Guide our feet into the way of peace.
- Make ready a people prepared for the coming of the Lord.

THEORY

Journal your thoughts on the following questions:

- How can your Aaronic Priesthood service prepare people in your family, quorum, and ward for a personal visit from Jesus Christ?
- What will you do to ensure that the days of your Aaronic Priesthood service are like the days of Oliver Cowdery—days that are "never to be forgotten?"

CHAPTER 3

Parenting Priesthood Potential

With All My Heart, Might, Mind, and Strength

Whereby shall I know this?

—LUKE 1:8

This chapter is written by me, a dad, and for me, a dad. If you are a young man or a young woman, some of this chapter may not seem to apply to you right now. But if you believe that your preparatory years are about learning to one day be an awesome mom or dad, I would encourage you to read this chapter anyway. Being a parent is a big deal, and it is worth every effort for you to learn and prepare to be a noble and honorable parent. Just as parents work to know what is best for their children, it can be immensely helpful for you to work to understand the needs of your parents so that you can help them in their divine role of raising up children prepared to go before the Lord. This chapter is written to give perspective to both preparing young men and women as well as their imperfect parents. My objective is to provide hope and confidence for both you and your parents as you work together to deliver the Lord's priesthood power to His children.

Like all fathers, I want so badly for my son to grow to be wiser, stronger, and more obedient than I am. I have such great love and high expectations for him. I cherish all the wonderful elements that make him special. I also see how he is just like me in many ways, both blessed with my strengths and at times seemingly cursed with my weaknesses and human frailties. With both potential and pitfalls around every turn, knowing how to lead you, our children, to discover and fill the measure of your unique creation is the greatest opportunity, responsibility, and challenge given to parents like me.

In seeking to understand how to parent your Aaronic Priesthood potential, we as parents can return to the life of John the Baptist and his parents, Zacharias and Elisabeth. John the Baptist is the ultimate Aaronic Priesthood holder. Who better to look to for priesthood insights than to the man who restored the preparatory priesthood to the earth and the parents who raised him?

As we return to the scene of John's annunciation, remember the faithfulness, obedience, and dedication of Zacharias and Elisabeth. Elisabeth was "of the daughters of Aaron," meaning that she was a literal descendant of Aaron and thus was capable of passing along the birthright required for Aaronic Priesthood ordination. In considering our own qualifications to parent powerful priesthood holders, we, like Elisabeth, should similarly reflect on our own heritage and the decisions that we and others who have gone before us have made that have brought us to this great place where we can even contemplate the solemn responsibility of bringing children into our families that are seeking after righteousness. Being cognizant of our heritage and the associated "birthright" that we possess can give confidence and purpose to our parenting.

Elisabeth and Zacharias were "both righteous before God, walking in all the commandments and ordinances of the Lord blameless" (Luke 1:6). We know that Elisabeth was barren and that both she and Zacharias were "now well stricken in years" (Luke 1:7). For Elisabeth to accomplish her desire to become a mother, the hand of God would be required. This miracle was finally confirmed by the angel Gabriel, who affirmed to Zacharias that the aged couple's prayers had been heard. By aligning ourselves with these faithful yet certainly overwhelmed parents, we can find poignant empathy for our own parental self-doubt.

When Zacharias first saw the angel, "he was troubled, and fear fell upon him" (Luke 1:12). Zacharias's fear of the angel's announcement was soon dispelled as the angel informed him of the tremendous influence his son, John, would have on the world and the role he would fulfill in Heavenly Father's plan.

The angel's revelation contained the promises that many would rejoice at his birth. It was promised that John would be "great in the sight of the Lord" and that he would be impeccably obedient, not drinking "wine nor strong drink" (Luke 1:15). Furthermore, the angel promised that he would be "filled with the Holy Ghost" (Luke 1:15) from his mother's womb (as would later be made evident when Elisabeth received a visit from Mary, who was pregnant with the Christ child). John's baby blessing was effectively foretold by Gabriel.

The angel prophesied further: "And many of the children of Israel shall he turn to the Lord their God. And he shall go before him in the spirit and power of Elias, to turn the hearts of the fathers to the children and the disobedient to the wisdom of the just; to make ready a people prepared for the Lord" (Luke 1:17).

As beautiful as these promises were to Zacharias, the angel immediately noted the disbelief in the elderly father to be when Zacharias questioned the prophecy: "Whereby shall I know this, for I am an old man, and my wife well stricken in years?" His words have also been translated as "How can I be sure of this?" (Luke 1:18 KJV; NIV).

Because of his disbelief in the Lord's ability to deliver the miracle of conception to the elderly couple, the annunciation of John would have to wait. Zacharias was silenced by the angel for many months until the baby's circumcision when the full miracle of John's birth was finally shared with the world.

I love Zacharias. I think that many of us are like him. As parents, we have felt the joy and gladness when receiving the news of a child to be born. We are filled with hope when we first cradle our precious babes and feel the power of their potential. But like Zacharias, our joy and hope can quickly be consumed by doubt and fear as we contemplate the implications of mortality and allow the adversary to place subtle limits on the hope that we hold for our children. Sadly, it does not take long to experience the perils of parenting where our hope and optimism are subtly suffocated by the acknowledgment of our own parental shortcomings as well as the fact that our children come with the same mortal nature that we possess.

Zacharias's disbelief was not in the promise of John's potential, but rather in the miraculous reality of John's conception. As parents of boys today, we often allow doubt, fear, and our own lack of understanding to creep in and cast shadows on the realization of the promised priesthood potential bestowed upon you. When promised that our Aaronic Priesthood holders possess the potential to make ready a people prepared for the Lord, it is easy to often express our doubt in the measure by which we underestimate that potential as we find ourselves focusing more on their frailties than on their features.

A few months before my son, Josh, turned eight years old, I had a sweet but simple experience in which the Lord offered me a moment of perspective on my own capability to either promote potential or to deliver doubt to the boy that I am responsible to raise. On a cold Sunday morning in late February, I walked with some trepidation into Josh's room to wake him for church. Josh is a great boy, but at that time he was a self-described "home-etarian." Sometimes Josh's interest in staying close to home would get in the way of our family's need to be other places, with church being chief among those.

On this winter day, knowing that Josh had stayed up late and that we had a 9:00 a.m. sacrament meeting, I approached gently to wake him. When I walked into the room, I found that he was already awake and sitting up in bed. We talked quietly for a minute before I gently asked him to get up and get ready for church. Different than many mornings, when I might have engaged in an agitated debate to convince him that it was in his best interest to trade his bed for a bench, I followed a prompting to approach this morning's invitation with gentleness and patience before quietly leaving him to decide for himself how he would respond to my invitation.

I left Josh still in bed with my request to get up and get ready for church. I returned a few minutes later to find a nearly dressed boy working hard to pull up his second sock. He proudly stood up, put his shoes on, and walked out ahead of me without saying a word. His silence was complemented by my own speechlessness as I tried to process this very unusual circumstance.

When he walked out of his room and down the hall, I saw a disheveled boy with his shirt only part-way tucked in and most of the way tucked out. I saw a belt that had missed at least one loop, leaving an inch of his white shirt showing between the bottom of his belt and the top of his pants. I saw a zipper-tie that was pulled snug against the skin of his neck, having never found the underside of his collar. As I sized him up in his brisk step down the hall, I noted a pant leg half-tucked into a sock. I saw tufts of his hair trying to find their place after being so abruptly removed from the pillow where they had been comfortably pasted just a few minutes before.

But most of all, in that moment as he walked from the hallway and across our living room, I saw a boy who, on that morning, recognized his duty to God, a boy simply trying to be like Jesus. I saw a boy preparing for baptismal and priesthood covenants. I saw a future missionary, a husband, and father. But most of all, I saw a disciple of Jesus Christ.

At times we may find ourselves like Zacharias, doubting the miracle that the Lord is working within our families. Zacharias doubted the miracle of John's conception. I doubted the miracle of getting to church on time without contention.

With our sons as babes in our arms, we may not question the miracle of conception like Zacharias, but in time, we are likely to catch ourselves questioning the priesthood potential of the boy with the bedhead.

We learn through experience that our children are children. Like us, they come programmed and predisposed to be "natural" men and women (see Mosiah 3:19). It does not take long to see that amidst all their potential they are apples that do not fall too far from the proverbial tree. We look at them and see ourselves. We see them experience many of the same challenges and struggles that we may be navigating, and in this, we see them fail to overcome that same natural man that so often afflicts each of us.

In my example, because I had grown accustomed to the stressful Sunday morning negotiation with Josh to get ready for church, I first approached him cautiously because I was not only familiar with his natural tendency to drag his feet on a Sunday morning, but I had also recognized that this really was not all that different from a similar negotiation that I regularly have with my own pillow. I saw my own struggles in his and recognized the personally familiar challenge of overcoming the natural man.

The daily difficulties that are merely part of parenting and family life are subtle in their capacity to be turned against the purposes of the Lord by strangling the powerful potential that our sons and daughters possess. Within the mundane, we barely notice the inklings of doubt that are easily introduced into our minds.

In this way, we as your parents, who have been entrusted to mentor and maximize what each son and daughter has to offer the world, are susceptible to inadvertently placing limitations on the priesthood potential within you, our sons and daughters, by failing to see you as the Lord sees you. We allow our own shortcomings to influence our expectations for the miraculous work in which we are privileged to take part.

Like Zacharias, in my moment of doubt on that February morning, I was also stricken with silence and was forced to only observe the miracle. Like the father of John the Baptist, in my moment of speechlessness, I was plagued with heavenly perspective.

I recognized that when I am calm and loving, I can learn gospel principles. I felt grateful for the Spirit of the Lord that helped me to be calm on that cold morning as I approached my son. In my quiet admiration, I was thankful to have been blessed to withhold any aggravation or frustration that often accompanied those chaotic Sunday mornings. I felt grateful for what I had been shown. I concluded that Josh and I are very much alike in how the Lord sees us both. We are both trying to follow Him. Even though we may both have our shirt figuratively untucked and have missed a couple of belt loops, He loves us, not for how we are, but for the level of our effort to come unto Him.

I felt a deep and overwhelming sense of gratitude for a loving Savior who gave me this moment to see this boy as He sees him. A boy who was discovering for himself how to follow the Lord. A boy who was making efforts in his own ways and according to his own capabilities to build a relationship with the Master. I felt an increased measure of responsibility to guard these moments, to not destroy them with anger, frustration, or impatience. I recognized in that moment how great the Lord's patience and love is for me as He sees me struggle to keep my own shirt tucked in and my belt properly threaded.

As you contemplate your own priesthood potential, I invite you to discuss with your parents your family's capacity to be blessed with priesthood power. You might pursue a transparent conversation with them to discuss what hopes they had for you when you were born. Invite them to share with you how they may have felt like Zacharias—overwhelmed with the gratitude for the blessing that you were as an unblemished babe in their arms and whether any feelings of their own inadequacy may have caused them to doubt what you could accomplish. Together you may look to identify how the Lord is sustaining them in their efforts to be the type of parents that can provide the right mortal experience for you, the one that will prepare you to be a powerful priesthood holder.

I invite your parents to be thoughtful as they consider both the miracle of your priesthood progress and of their progress as parents. I hope that you will have humility to consider all the ways that they are like Zacharias and Elisabeth—filled with both faith and even a little bit of fear. I hope your parents will be open to evaluating their doubts and fears, but also that they will be quick to remember their righteousness and obedience, as well as yours. You may also look to be open about what you can do to help them in this daunting but divine calling of sustaining a powerful priesthood. I hope that you might remove your own day-to-day dynamics and look objectively at the task that your family has to contribute children to the Lord who can bear the gospel standard. I hope that together you will see the clear influence of the Savior and His Atonement in your family's life to sustain and uplift both you and your parents in the collective effort required to parent your priesthood potential. Finally, like Zacharias and Elisabeth, your parents should be confident in knowing that their faithfulness, and even their fears, can qualify them for the miracle and blessing of participating in the powerful process of raising children ready to fulfill their duties to make ready a people prepared for the coming of the Lord.

PARENTING PRIESTHOOD POTENTIAL

With All My Heart, Might, Mind, and Strength

DOCTRINE

Read "The Family: A Proclamation to the World."
Look for the specific responsibilities that are given to parents to fulfill Heavenly Father's plan for families.

Review Luke 1.
Look for the verses in which Zacharias and Elisabeth showed both fear and faith as they received the responsibility of being parents.

PRINCIPLE

Discuss with your parents how they have felt both confidence and fear in their sacred roles as a mother and father.

- Ask your parents what they have done to overcome their moments of doubt or fear in their role as your mother and father.
- Ask them how priesthood power has helped them to have courage like Elisabeth and Zacharias to love you with all their heart, might, mind, and strength.

THEORY

Journal your thoughts on the following questions:

- What are the attributes that you believe are important to develop to become an honorable mother or father?
- Write down at least three things that you can do now to prepare to be a worthy parent.

CHAPTER 4

Keys of the Preparatory Priesthood

I Will Love God, Keep My Covenants, and Use His Priesthood to Serve Others, Beginning in My Own Home

---

Upon you my fellow servants, in the name of Messiah I confer the Priesthood of Aaron, which holds the keys of the ministering of angels, and of the gospel of repentance, and of baptism by immersion for the remission of sins.

—DOCTRINE AND COVENANTS 13:1

I live near the Utah State Developmental Center and occasionally have the opportunity to attend sacrament meeting with the residents. (The Developmental Center provides resources and support for people with the most acute or complex disabilities. Most of the residents cannot speak or feed themselves.) On my most recent visit there, I witnessed some angelic Aaronic Priesthood holders extend special invitations to come unto Christ as they anxiously administered the sacrament.

That Sunday, I noticed a few of the higher-functioning male residents were able to help with the blessing and passing of the sacrament. I will not soon forget the innocent enthusiasm that filled their service that morning. I gained a renewed perspective for what it means to love God by being anxiously engaged as I watched them use His priesthood service to serve others.

The blessing of the sacrament was almost unintelligible as men with severe speech impediments recited the sacrament prayer. Clarity of speech, however, was not needed to hear the tongues of angels speak these words.

As the men passed the sacrament, they handed the tray to the person at the end of the row before they enthusiastically proclaimed, in very loud voices, things like, "Let's dooo this," "You got this," and "Perfeeeect!" Then, after handing the tray, they would literally run around the back of the chairs to be available to pick up the tray as it reached the end of the row. As they reached to receive the tray, they would eagerly and innocently ask, again out loud, "Anybody else?" or "Did you get some?"

Soon the bread tray came to me. With a smile on my face, I felt the sincerity of their invitations. They spoke as if they knew that they were delivering something that would truly bring life-giving sustenance to each of us who were there to partake of the sacred emblems. I reached for the bread and noticed that the piece of bread that I partook had been broken by hands less concerned with efficiency and more concerned with ensuring that each person had enough.

As I partook of the sacrament that day, I was overcome with the magnitude of my covenants and a uniquely new desire to align myself with the Savior. That morning, I had been expounded, exhorted, warned, and most of all invited to come unto Christ by these ministering angels of the Lord.

I left that meeting with a renewed outlook for the Aaronic Priesthood's role in administering the sacrament. I asked myself, do we, as both Aaronic Priesthood holders and partakers of the sacrament, have the same understanding and enthusiasm for the emblems and unifying experience that we are delivering as ministers, administers, and partakers of the Atonement of Jesus Christ?

Amidst all of their mortal deficiencies, the men who offered me the sacrament were blessed with an increased capability to minister to me. These Aaronic Priesthood holders had delivered on the same sacred mission given to John the Baptist to give each individual an opportunity to accept the knowledge of salvation by the remission of their sins and to give light to those of us in darkness.

With agency as the governing principle of the universe, God's children must choose for themselves to accept the gospel. This requires that each child of God be given an individual opportunity to accept the invitation to receive the gospel and its saving ordinances. Because of the one-by-one nature of this invitation, our Heavenly Father has authorized His priesthood authority to be utilized by those who serve Him for the purposes of delivering the gospel of Jesus Christ to His children that they might choose to be His disciples and qualify themselves for exaltation.

The pattern for the delivery of Christ's gospel was established in the most ancient of times when God taught Adam and Eve the plan of salvation and gave them priesthood keys and ordinances to enable their eternal progression and safe return to His presence. Leveraging their God-given agency, the adversary countered with offerings of his own as he sought to claim the hearts of God's children.

Following Cain's betrayal of his brother Abel, works of darkness began to prevail among God's children. Angry with the wicked, who "would not hearken unto his voice, nor believe on his Only Begotten Son" (Moses 5:57), our Heavenly Father cursed the earth and in His infinite love introduced the gospel of Jesus Christ and prepared a way for it to be preached to His children. As you read these verses from the Pearl of Great Price, look for three ways that Heavenly Father used to preach His gospel and how those teachings were confirmed to Adam. Finally, note for how long this gospel and these methods of preaching and confirming eternal truths were set forth to be employed on the earth:

> And thus the Gospel began to be preached, from the beginning, being declared *by holy angels sent forth from the presence of God, and by his own voice,* and *by the gift of the Holy Ghost. And thus all things were confirmed unto Adam, by an ordinance* and the Gospel preached, and a decree sent forth, *that it should be in the world, until the end thereof;* and thus it was. (Moses 5:58–59; emphasis added)

I love reading about Adam and Eve. We can learn a lot about our Heavenly Father's nature and manner of teaching His children by paying attention to how our first parents were given the gospel. In this verse, a loving Heavenly Father outlines the method by which the gospel would be preached from the beginning of time until the very end of the world. He identifies three specific methods:

1. By holy angels sent forth from the presence of God.
2. By His own voice (through the prophets; see Amos 3:7, D&C 1:38).
3. By the gift of the Holy Ghost.

By establishing His gospel on a foundation of prophets, revelation, and priesthood authority, God has ensured that the saving principles and ordinances of the gospel of Jesus Christ will be available individually to all of His children. These methods are eternal and have been employed whenever prophets have been on the earth.

On May 15, 1829, near Harmony, Pennsylvania, following centuries of apostasy in which priesthood authority was not present on the earth, John the Baptist conferred upon Joseph and Oliver the Aaronic Priesthood. In that moment he declared the restoration of Aaronic Priesthood keys, which re-enabled the continued one-by-one preaching of the gospel of Jesus Christ and the realization of its associated ordinances and covenants. The restoration of this preparatory priesthood provided God's children with the necessary keys and authority to prepare each of them to receive the Savior.

The Doctrine and Covenants captures the moment of the restoration of the Aaronic Priesthood in a single verse in section 13 and declares that the following priesthood keys are to remain on the earth until a future time when the sons of Levi will reclaim their ancient birthright:

- Keys of the ministering of angels.
- Keys of the gospel of repentance and of baptism by immersion for the remission of sins.

When considering the role of angels in delivering the message of the gospel, both anciently with Adam and in this dispensation with John the Baptist, it becomes critical to understand how these Aaronic Priesthood keys function to accomplish God's purpose of bringing to pass the immortality and eternal life of man. I remember as a young deacon first being introduced to Doctrine and Covenants 13 and getting through the first elegant line: "Upon you my fellow servants, in the name of Messiah, I confer upon you the Priesthood of Aaron." While this language was clear, I was somewhat confounded as I glossed over the lines about ministering angels and keys to the gospel of repentance and of baptism before getting completely lost in something about an offering to be made by the sons of Levi.

Aaronic Priesthood keys were not easy concepts for my twelve-year-old mind to understand. The concept of ministering angels as it related to my everyday experience was very foreign to me. While other concepts such as the nature of the Holy Ghost began to resonate over time, the role of ministering angels never seemed to align well with my own gospel experiences. Adolescence and a mission offered tangible experiences with repentance and baptism, but understanding how all the keys work together proved to be a more difficult task.

Over time, some questions began to crystallize around these Aaronic Priesthood keys: What does it really mean to have keys to the ministering of angels? Angels seemed to have a prominent role throughout Christianity, but I struggled to understand whether they really had a role in my everyday life as a follower of the restored gospel. Repentance and baptism were a bit more tangible, but still I wondered whether these Aaronic Priesthood keys were all separate in purpose and unique unto themselves, or did they somehow work together to accomplish a combined purpose for the Lord?

For many of us, our initial inclination is to try to understand each of these priesthood keys individually. We seek to understand each key as separate and distinct from the other as if they are only designed to unlock uniquely different doors. In reality, while distinct, these keys work in unison to bring people to Christ and are most easily understood when viewed together through the lens of their collective purpose.

Simply stated, the purpose of the Aaronic Priesthood keys is to enable the unification of God's children with Jesus Christ—to make ready a people prepared for the coming of the Lord.

The Book of Mormon teaches that the purpose of angels and

their ministry is to lead men and women to faith, prompting within them a desire to not only believe in Christ, but moreover, to be like Christ. This transformation is only fully realized through the gospel of repentance and is consummated, or made eternal, through the Aaronic Priesthood ordinances of baptism and subsequently renewed through the sacrament.

In the final pages of the Book of Mormon, the prophet Moroni records the words of his father, Mormon, who offered beautiful insights into how the authority provided by the keys of the Aaronic Priesthood enable God's children to access the power of that priesthood to become unified with the Savior. Specifically, in Moroni 7, Mormon gives a beautiful sermon on the role of angels. Here he outlines very clearly how the key of the ministry of angels works together with the keys of the gospel of repentance and baptism to enable each of us to become like the Savior as we partake of His Atonement.

Mormon begins by explaining what God accomplished through the ministering of angels in ancient times: "Wherefore, by the ministering of angels, and by every word which proceeded forth out of the mouth of God, men began to exercise faith in Christ; and thus by faith, they did lay hold upon every good thing; and thus it was until the coming of Christ" (Moroni 7:25).

Consider the ancient times to which Mormon refers in verse 25. He references the time before Christ, when the Aaronic Priesthood was on the earth. In those days, the ministering of angels contributed to men's ability to exercise faith. Confirming God's method of using angels to preach the gospel, we can identify many examples in the scriptures where the ministry of angels promoted the faith and repentance of God's children. A few examples include the angel who ministered to Daniel by closing the mouths of the lions to protect him, which further strengthened the faith of the influential King Darius, who subsequently promoted the God of Daniel throughout his kingdom; the angel who ministered to Alma the Younger and the sons of Mosiah by calling them to repentance; or even the angel Gabriel who visited Zacharias and exercised Aaronic Priesthood keys to remove doubt and promote the faith of the father of John the Baptist.

The role of angels to promote humanity's exercise of faith in Christ becomes more relevant to our day when paired with the fourth Article of Faith in which members of the Church declare that faith in the Lord Jesus Christ is the first principle of the gospel. If we pay attention, we see how the ministering of angels worked in ancient times to enable believers to find faith in Jesus Christ and thus embrace the first principle of the preparatory gospel.

In this same verse in Moroni 7, we begin to see the Lord shine light on the purposes of the Aaronic Priesthood that can be applied in our day with references to the combined keys of ministering angels and the preparatory gospel and their combined purpose to first establish faith in Jesus Christ among God's children. In fact, Moroni is explicit in teaching about the "office" of angels called to minister. As you read this passage, look for the following:

- To whom angels show themselves.
- Three purposes of the ministry assigned to the angels.

> For he [the Savior] hath answered the ends of the law, and he claimeth all those who have faith in him.
>
> And because he hath done this, my beloved brethren, have miracles ceased? Behold I say unto you, Nay; neither have angels ceased to minister unto the children of men. For behold they are subject unto him to minister according to the word of his command, showing themselves unto them of strong faith and a firm mind in every form of godliness. And the office of their ministry is *to call men unto repentance, and to fulfill and to do the work of the covenants* of the Father, which he hath made unto the children of men *to prepare the way* among the children of men, by *declaring the word of Christ unto the* ***chosen vessels*** *of the Lord,* that they may bear testimony of him. (Moroni 7:28, 29–31; emphasis added)

We can glean some important truths from Mormon's teachings: Angels continue to be a relevant resource for the Savior's ministry to His children. They minister unto those who qualify—even in our day. Those who qualify for the ministry of angels have strong faith and are of a firm mind in every form of godliness. The recipients of the ministry of angels are called "chosen vessels."

The office of an angel's ministry is to call men unto repentance, to do the work of the covenants of the Father, and to prepare the way by declaring the words of Christ unto the chosen vessels so that they may bear testimony of Him.

The scripture articulates further that angels minister unto those who qualify "in every form of godliness." Remember from Doctrine and Covenants 84 that "the power of godliness is manifest in the ordinances of the priesthood." Mormon suggests that the ministering of angels comes to those of strong faith and a firm mind "by way of the ordinances of the priesthood," which thus fulfill God's purposes of bringing salvation to His children.

Who are these chosen vessels that are blessed by this ministry of the angels? Are not the chosen vessels those who are "of strong faith and a firm mind in every form of godliness"? Are not the chosen vessels those who are actively pursuing the covenants of the Father seeking priesthood power in their lives? Effectively, are not the chosen vessels those who have the testimony of Jesus and who are working to follow Him? To me these chosen vessels are simply the members of our wards and branches who are already under covenant to seek the Savior by striving to be worthy to take the sacrament each week as administered by faithful Aaronic Priesthood holders.

When we, as followers of Jesus Christ, recognize Aaronic Priesthood holders as those charged with preparing the way for each of us, as the "chosen vessels" to be of strong faith, firm minds, and to be filled with testimony, we will come to know full well the power and purpose of this preparatory priesthood.

To me, this suggests that those who have strong faith and who are firm in their commitment to pursue priesthood ordinances can expect to be accompanied by literal angels. The role of these angels is to inspire faith sufficient for God's children to have a desire to repent that they may realize the full healing, redeeming, and enabling power of the Atonement that awaits as they receive the saving ordinances of the gospel. In this way, the Lord opens the door for His chosen vessels to receive priesthood power, or the power of godliness, through the preparatory keys of the Aaronic Priesthood.

If we safely include ourselves in this group of chosen vessels, these verses come to life. First, Mormon explains that through their angelic ministry, Aaronic priesthood bearers prepare the way among the children of men by declaring the word of Christ, that the chosen vessels of the Lord "may bear testimony of him" (Moroni 7:31). Then, in the next verse, and in a spectacular way, Mormon teaches clearly how these keys to the preparatory priesthood unlock the access to the gospel, not just for the chosen vessels but for all of God's children. Here he beautifully explains with whom these "chosen vessels" will be prepared to share their testimony of Christ. As you read this verse, consider who Mormon is referencing as "the residue of men": "And by so doing, the Lord God prepareth the way that the residue of men may have faith in Christ, that the Holy Ghost may have a place in their hearts, according to the power thereof; *and after this manner bringeth to pass the Father the covenants which he hath made unto the children of men*" (Moroni 7:32; emphasis added).

Wow! Did you follow all of that? Let's put it all together. Angels are called by God to minister to the Lord's chosen vessels. This could be you and I who are under covenant, being of strong faith and a firm mind. They minister to us "in every form of godliness," or as we know it through the ordinances of the preparatory gospel—in effect, through baptism and the renewing power of the sacrament. By virtue of receiving the Holy Ghost, we too can access these ministering angels who can enable us to speak the words of Christ, just as they have spoken to us.

We can bear testimony of the Savior and strengthen one another as chosen vessels. We also qualify ourselves to participate in the preparation of the "residue of men" for them to receive the covenant. Who are the residue of men? They are everyone else—all of the rest of God's children. The residue of men is those who are not acquainted with the preparatory gospel of Jesus Christ. These are those who await the words of Christ and the influence of the Holy Ghost as delivered by the chosen vessels and angels of the Lord, who being under covenant are able to speak by the power of the Holy Ghost.

Under the keys of the Aaronic Priesthood, covenant men and women have a royal opportunity to receive the ministering of angels and to bear testimony of Him as we prepare ourselves within our homes and wards to take the Father's covenant to all of His children. Through this preparatory process, as chosen vessels, we can prepare ourselves to later operate under the greater Melchizedek Priesthood keys, which include the Melchizedek Priesthood mission of taking the gospel to all the world. In this way the Lord perpetuates a process of identifying and inviting chosen vessels to come unto Christ, accept His gospel, and receive His covenant. Through the keys of the Aaronic Priesthood, the gathering of Israel is instigated.

How is this accomplished? Consider the role that families and Aaronic Priesthood holders can have in activating these keys together within their own homes and wards. Members of the Church become saints as they accept the preparatory gospel and are baptized. They function in their families, serving one another and preparing for the sacrament each week. The bishop oversees the administration of the sacrament. He ensures that the work of this covenant is administered with the dignity that the Savior's Atonement deserves. He is entrusted to ensure that all within his stewardship who partake of the sacrament do so worthily. He does this by leaning on those who hold Aaronic Priesthood duties to call families unto repentance.

As family members bind together and respond to the gentle calls to repentance, and as they participate in the ordinances administered within the ward, their testimonies are strengthened. As they persist in their consistency and sincerity to follow the Savior, they come to know Him. Through their commitment to the gospel of Jesus Christ, they are able to partake of the Atonement and be changed to become like Him. In time, their testimonies grow to where they are confident and firm in their personal witness of the Savior. Their unique life experiences have allowed them to come to know the Savior, and they soon have a desire to share that witness of hope and peace with others. In my experience, these moments of unification with the Savior are what prompt people to have a desire to serve the Lord in various forms of missionary service. As the youth of the noble birthright, it should be your highest goal to seek this unification with the Savior and the conversion to His gospel.

As members respond to these promptings to proclaim the gospel through missionary work, the residue of men is soon exposed to the gospel of Jesus Christ, that ultimately the Holy Ghost may have a place in their hearts as well. It is the deep and abiding testimony acquired by virtue of the activation of Aaronic Priesthood keys that prepares all of God's children for the opportunity to accept the gospel of Jesus Christ and to embrace both the covenants of the Aaronic and Melchizedek priesthood. In this way, all of God's children will be given an opportunity to experiment on His word to develop their own personal witness of Jesus Christ.

Finally, as Aaronic Priesthood holders fulfill their duties in this sacred process, they in turn prepare the way for themselves to be part of this great movement to share their testimony of Jesus Christ throughout the world—to "the residue of men." Is it, therefore, any wonder why our modern-day prophets and apostles boldly declare that every able young man should prepare to serve a mission?

Mormon's delineation of the ministry of angels is magnificent. Herein, Mormon perceptively foretells the Aaronic Priesthood roles of deacons, teachers, priests, and bishops, and gives purpose to their duties within the restored Church of Jesus Christ. These verses should give powerful purpose to you as a holder of the Aaronic Priesthood. In literal application, an Aaronic Priesthood holder empowered by priesthood keys through the gift of the Holy Ghost is entrusted with the words of Christ. As they share the words of Christ through the fulfillment of their priesthood duties, they enable others to experience the power, or influence of, the Holy Ghost as spoken by angels on the Lord's errand.

In a modern-day ward, it is often the angels of the Aaronic Priesthood who fulfill the office of their angelic ministry to call men unto repentance, to do the work of the covenants of the Father, and ultimately to prepare the way for the chosen vessels to bear testimony of Jesus Christ.

Take a moment and contemplate with me how the ministry of angels functions within a ward operating under Aaronic Priesthood keys with a quorum whose duties dovetail with the primary functions of ministering angels as outlined by Mormon.

> **BISHOPS:** "The bishop's duty is to be a judge in Israel . . . to judge his people by the testimony of the just, and by the assistance of his counselors, according to the laws of the kingdom which are given by the prophets of God (D&C 58:17–18). Think about the bishop as he as he meets with those preparing for baptism or those who are working to repent and return to the sacrament table. In ministering to a ward member challenged by sin or other situations creating distance between the Lord and His children, is the bishop not preaching the words of Christ and inviting that child of God to repent? Is not this fulfilling and doing the work of the covenants?
>
> **DEACONS:** "A deacon's duty is to warn, expound, exhort, and teach, and invite all to come unto Christ" (D&C 20:59). Think of the deacons as they pass the sacrament. Are they not extending invitations to repent and to come unto Christ through the renewal of a covenant? A deacon's "work" to pass the sacrament warns, expounds, exhorts, and teaches the covenant as men and women are invited to come unto Christ by partaking of the Lord's sacred emblems. The deacon's shirt and tie and reverent demeanor serve as a quiet voice of *warning* for ward members to not partake of the sacrament unworthily. As he extends a tray, he *exhorts* members of the Lord's church to come unto Him again by partaking of the sacred emblems. In so doing, he also *expounds* the doctrines of the Atonement of Jesus Christ to the covenant member who is thoughtfully contemplating the Lord's sacrifice. A deacon's work should never be deemed as menial. His task is truly to do the work of the covenants.

TEACHERS: "The teacher's duty is to watch over the church always, and be with and strengthen them; and see that there is no iniquity in the church, neither hardness with each other, neither lying, backbiting, nor evil speaking; and see that the church meet together often, and also see that all the members do their duty" (D&C 20:53–55). With some guidance by a mindful bishop, even a teacher assigned to serve as an usher can fulfill his purpose to "watch over the church . . . and to see that there is no iniquity" therein by welcoming members and visitors with a handshake and a smile that encourages them to prepare and partake worthily of the Lord's supper. Is not a warm handshake and the invitation to reverently find a seat in the chapel an invitation to repent, renew covenants, and to bear testimony of Jesus Christ?

Additionally, when teachers prepare the sacrament in a reverent and orderly fashion, they quietly teach younger deacons about the sacred nature of the sacramental emblems. Even through the simple manner that they place the cloth over the prepared sacramental altar, they set the tone for the ordinance that the deacons will deliver and through their example fulfill their duty to teach about the reverence required of the watchful deacons as they invite the congregation to come unto Christ.

PRIESTS: "The priest's duty is to preach, teach, expound, exhort, and baptize, and administer the sacrament, and visit the house of each member, and exhort them to pray vocally and in secret and attend to all family duties" (D&C 20:46–47). Think of the priests who administer the outward ordinance of the sacrament and whose duty it is to baptize. The angelic work of the covenants they perform is obvious. Consider how the reverent recitation of the sacrament prayer *teaches* and *exhorts* you and I as we repent and renew our covenants with God.

Both teachers and priests share another important duty to minister as part of their duties to preach, teach, watch over the Church, and visit the house of each member. I cannot think of a more angelic ministry than to fulfill this assignment. Is not this the work that, when properly administered, can inspire individuals and families to accept the invitation to come unto Christ and prepare themselves to receive and renew their covenants with the Father? Furthermore, is not this the work that will prepare these chosen vessels of the Aaronic Priesthood for a future day when they will take this same ministry to the residue of men?

Reflect again on those angelic ministers who administered the emblems of the sacrament at the Utah State Developmental Center. They exemplified an understanding of God's ministerial methods to deliver the covenant and extend the invitation to accept the gospel and come unto Christ. Think about how you, in your own reverent way, can convey your understanding of the Aaronic Priesthood keys as you fulfill your duties within your own priesthood office.

In the October 2008 general conference, Elder Holland taught about the ministry of angels in this way:

> From the beginning down through the dispensations, God has used angels as His emissaries in conveying love and concern for His children. . . . Usually such beings are not seen. Sometimes they are. But seen or unseen they are always near. Sometimes their assignments are very grand and have significance for the whole world. Sometimes the messages are more private. Occasionally the angelic purpose is to warn. But most often it is to comfort, to provide some form of merciful attention, guidance in difficult times.[1]

As you consider Elder Holland's teachings, reflect for a moment on Nephi's words regarding angels and their means of communication: "Angels speak by the power of the Holy Ghost; wherefore, they speak the words of Christ. Wherefore, I said unto you, feast upon the words of Christ; for behold, the words of Christ will tell you all things what ye should do." (2 Nephi 32:2–3).

Here, Nephi states that the power by which angels speak is, in fact, by the power of the Holy Ghost. From this verse, I might suggest that angels carry with them the distinguished assignment to possess and transfer *the influence* of the Holy Ghost to God's children throughout the world.

When God's children feel the influence of the Holy Ghost, they are actually hearing or feeling words being spoken by literal angels. When these angels deliver the words of Christ and invite us to follow Him, it is by that sacred power of the Holy Ghost. Why is the Book of Mormon so powerful? Because it contains the words of Christ that when read and pondered, or rather "feasted upon," allow for the keys of the Aaronic Priesthood to be activated, beginning when ministering angels convey truth and invite obedience through the power of the Holy Ghost. This effort to "feast upon the words of Christ" alone can be sufficient to initiate the process of partaking of the Atonement of Jesus Christ.

As Nephi observed, one who has been confirmed and received the gift of the Holy Ghost can even qualify themselves to speak as the angels do by this same power. Missionaries regularly invite people to recognize the influence of the Holy Ghost as they are taught the gospel. It is reasonable to me to believe that the influence of the Holy Ghost so often felt by those receiving the missionary lessons is, in fact, delivered by angels. Whether they are angels dressed in white shirts and ties or those of the more heavenly variety, both are sent to minister unto God's children, even delivering the words of Christ by the power of the Holy Ghost.

Furthermore, when even a child receives the gift of the Holy Ghost following baptism, they are subsequently qualified to speak with this same tongue of angels, or in other words to be literal bearers of the same message of hope and happiness—even angels themselves. Consider the potential this truth offers you to exercise Aaronic Priesthood power within your own home. You have literally been empowered to speak with the tongue of angels. Because baptism and confirmation are given to all who exercise faith unto repentance, the ability to draw on the power of the Aaronic Priesthood—to speak with the tongues of angels—is priesthood power that is also available to all, both men and women, in Christ's kingdom.

Your home may be filled with this gift of ministering angels to speak truth, to comfort, to protect, and to invite you and your family members to come unto Christ. As a holder of the Aaronic Priesthood, you can live the Young Men's theme as you love God and keep His covenants so that you are able to effectively use His priesthood to serve others, beginning in your own home.

Within your ward or branch, as you prepare, bless, or pass the sacrament (or even as you serve in less obvious roles, such as an usher in sacrament meeting), you deliver on your divinely appointed duties as revealed in the Restoration and fulfill the purposes of your angelic ministry. Whether by warning, expounding, exhorting, watching over, preaching, or teaching, an Aaronic Priesthood holder has the charge to assist his family and lead God's children to repent of their sins, or more broadly to invite them to change their character through the Atonement of Jesus Christ. Imperative to God's children receiving their saving ordinances are the keys of the Aaronic Priesthood, humbly activated as deacons, teachers, priests, and bishops fulfill their sacred duties.

As you contemplate the majesty of the keys to the ministry of angels, I hope you will feel within your soul a sense of the comprehensive nature of God's plan. I hope that you will see clearly that YOU have an important part in that plan. I hope that you will feel of Christ's love for all of His children, of His deep love for you, and of His need for you to help deliver His love to others through the effective activation of the Aaronic Priesthood keys to which you have access.

Aaronic Priesthood keys are the keys to a very powerful engine that when firing on all cylinders will power the vehicle that will carry Christ's Atonement to all of His children. This vehicle is a very big bus with room enough for all. However, if, as Aaronic Priesthood holders, we fail to engage the keys and turn the ignition, the engine will never fire, and God's children will be left standing at the bus stop.

Equipped with an understanding of the Aaronic Priesthood keys to the ministry of angels and the preparatory gospel, each of us can identify ways by which we can both be strengthened by Aaronic Priesthood keys and by which we can strengthen and enable others as we work to sustain one another in our own personal pursuit of repentance and to do the work of the covenants.

While heavenly messengers stand ready to wield the power of heaven, it is the holders of the Aaronic Priesthood, who along with all covenanted members of Christ's Church, are called to act in the office of this ministry of angels. It is the duty of deacons, teachers, priests, and bishops, along with those who serve under their stewardship, to call men unto repentance, to fulfill and to do the work of the covenants. Like John the Baptist in ancient times, it is the duty of those who both hold and sustain the Aaronic Priesthood to prepare the way for the coming of the Lord. It is their duty to declare the word of Christ unto the chosen vessels of the Lord that they may bear testimony of him, that the residue of men may have faith in Christ—so that one day, as Joseph Smith stated, "The purposes of God shall be accomplished and the Great Jehovah shall say the work is done!"[2]

NOTES

1. Elder Jeffrey R. Holland, "The Ministry of Angels," *Ensign*, Nov. 2008, 29.
2. Moroni 7:32 and Joseph Smith's Wentworth Letter (1842). See goodreads.com/quotes/295088-the-standard-of-truth-has-been-erected-no-unhallowed-hand. Accessed May 22, 2020.

KEYS OF THE PREPARATORY PRIESTHOOD

I Will Love God, Keep My Covenants, and Use His Priesthood to Serve Others, Beginning in My Own Home

---

DOCTRINE

Read: Moroni 7:25, 31–32; 2 Nephi 32:2–3; Doctrine and Covenants 20:46–47, 53–55, 59; 58:17–18.

- Identify at least three roles assigned to ministering angels.
- Identify how angels communicate with us.
- Identify the specific duties of each Aaronic Priesthood office.

PRINCIPLE

Lead a discussion with your quorum or family to counsel together about the following:

- The ways you see modern Aaronic Priesthood offices exercising the keys of the ministry of angels both in their homes and wards to:
    - Call men unto repentance.
    - Do the work of the covenants.
    - Prepare the way by declaring the words of Christ unto the chosen vessels.

THEORY

Journal what you can do in your current priesthood office within your home to:

- Love God.
- Keep your covenants.
- Use His priesthood to serve others.

With your quorum identify what you can do to declare Christ's words and effect the ministry of angels within your family, ward, or branch.

CHAPTER 5

The Gospel of Repentance and Baptism

As I Strive to Serve, Exercise Faith, Repent, and Improve Each Day

---

Which gospel is the gospel of repentance and of baptism, and the remission of sins.

—DOCTRINE AND COVENANTS 84:27

Once while serving as a bishop, I had a young family come in for tithing settlement. They had an especially cute and precocious little girl who was about four years old at the time. As we wrapped up our visit, I could tell that this little girl had a pressing question. She slowly walked up to me with a very curious look in her eyes and asked, "Do bishops have sharp teeth?" Of course, her parents and I erupted in laughter.

I have reflected periodically on that question and what I might have done to have earned this innocent and sincere inquiry. Bishops have an important role in serving as judges in Israel. They are set apart to evaluate and mentor our individual preparation to commune with Christ through the preparatory ordinances of baptism and the sacrament. Most bishops likely do not have sharp teeth. However, for many, the times when we need the help of a common judge can feel as frightening as meeting a man with carnivorous canines. Through great experience, it has long been proven that those who sincerely pursue this path of repentance will learn that a common judge is a loving judge who assists us in accessing the Savior's Atonement.

Doctrine and Covenants 107 calls attention to a sacred Aaronic Priesthood role that is held specifically by bishops—that of being a judge in Israel: "And also to be a judge in Israel, to do the business of the church, to sit in judgment upon transgressors upon testimony as it shall be laid before him according to the laws, by the assistance of his counselors, whom he has chosen or will choose among the elders of the church. This is the duty of a bishop who is not a literal descendant of Aaron, but has been ordained to the High Priesthood after the order of Melchizedek" (D&C 107:72–73).

Serving in the capacity of a judge in Israel, by all accounts, can be a lonely post—just ask a bishop's wife what it can be like late on a Sunday afternoon when her husband stumbles through the door carrying the burdens of the ward. Though the assignment is taxing, a bishop is buoyed up as he leans on the priesthood keys of the ministry of angels and the preparatory gospel of repentance and baptism to fulfill his duty to God.

While the gospel of repentance is a deeply personal and individual pursuit, a bishop can best fulfill his role as a judge in Israel when he looks to administer that gospel by leveraging the priesthood service rendered within all three Aaronic Priesthood quorums over which he has stewardship. As an Aaronic Priesthood holder, have you ever thought that you might have a role in helping a bishop administer repentance to the members of your ward? Could it be possible that when John the Baptist conferred the keys of the gospel of repentance, he intended those keys to be used by more than just a bishop?

In the Church of Jesus Christ today, we regularly acknowledge the bishop as the holder of the keys to the gospel of repentance. At times, it seems that our repentant culture points to the bishop's office as the isolated island that each must swim to alone. However, this line of thinking can disallow a repentant person from accessing the full power of the bishop's Aaronic Priesthood role to administer the gospel of repentance and baptism by limiting the participation in and acknowledgment of the Aaronic Priesthood service rendered by each quorum in their own respective capacity to do the work of the covenants.

To better evaluate the administration of the gospel of repentance and baptism, we can again consider the related duties associated with each Aaronic Priesthood office. Among the Aaronic Priesthood duties outlined in the Doctrine and Covenants are the following:

> The *priest's* duty is to preach, teach, expound, exhort, and baptize, and administer the sacrament, and visit the house of each member and exhort them to pray vocally and in secret and attend to all family duties. And he may also ordain other priests, teachers, and deacons. (D&C 20:46–48; emphasis added)

> The *teacher's* duty is to watch over the church always, and be with and strengthen them; And see that there is no iniquity in the church, neither hardness with each other, neither lying, backbiting nor evil speaking; And see that the church meet together often, and also see that all members do their duty. And is to be assisted always, in all his duties in the church by the *deacons,* if occasions requires. But neither teachers nor deacons have authority to baptize, administer the sacrament, or lay on hands; They are however, to warn, expound, exhort, and teach, and invite all to come unto Christ. (D&C 20:53–55; 57–59; emphasis added)

Consider also the ways in which these three priesthood offices (deacon, teacher, priest,) work together to support the bishop in his role as a judge in Israel. To begin, we should ask ourselves, what is a common judge? A common judge is one who is called to minister and evaluate the state of preparation of those who desire to make or renew covenants with the Lord. In this capacity, the bishop's role is to help people repent of their sins and obtain forgiveness from the Lord. The bishop is entrusted to represent the Lord and to protect all His interests, including His interest to bring salvation to His children. The bishop is to safeguard the saving ordinances of baptism and the sacrament, ensuring that they are administered only when a person is well-prepared to be blessed by their power.

The Bible Dictionary explains ministry as follows:

> The work of the ministry is to do the work of the Lord on the earth—to represent the Lord among the people, preach the gospel, and administer the ordinances thereof." This definition points to a minister as one who is "called of God, as was Aaron" (Heb.5:4), and endowed with the holy priesthood, represents the Lord when he is performing his official duties and is the Lord's agent. Therefore, what he does "according to the will of the Lord is the Lord's business" (D&C 64:29). The Lord has given apostles, prophets, evangelists, high priests, seventies, elders, bishops, priests, teachers, deacons, helps, and governments for the perfecting of the saints, for the work of the ministry, for the edifying of the body of Christ" (the Church), until all have reached the spiritual stature of Christ, the whole body being 'fitly joined together' by that which every part supplieth. (Bible Dictionary—Ministry)

While the tasks of counseling and ministering to individuals as they partake of Christ's Atonement are uniquely led by the bishop, it is also within the capacity of deacons, teachers, priests, and "helps"—which can be easily interpreted to include young sisters assigned to minister in Aaronic Priesthood assignments, to assist far more than they often realize. Along with these sisters, priesthood holders of these lesser offices can assist the bishop as they fulfill their priesthood duties and place baptism and the sacrament in their place of preeminence as the capstone ordinances for all the Saints who seek the Lord's mercy within His preparatory gospel.

It is worth acknowledging the ability that young women have to harness these keys to the ministry of angels. Young women can and do receive ministering assignments similar to those given to those young men who hold offices in the Aaronic Priesthood. As covenant members of Christ's church and operating under the same Aaronic Priesthood keys held by the bishop, young women similarly have full access to the ministry of angels. They are equally eligible to receive messages from the tongues of angels through the Holy Ghost, enabling them to be effective ministers on the behalf of the Lord. I have seen this transpire in my own ward where young women are assigned to join the priests on visits to individuals who are homebound and unable to get to church to partake of the sacrament. These young women come prepared with a gospel message. They effectuate the keys of the ministering of angels by inviting members to come unto Christ as they partake of the sacrament that is prepared and blessed by the priests. They have an important place in harnessing the keys of the Aaronic Priesthood.

To better understand how Aaronic Priesthood offices can work together to enable access to the Atonement, we can again look to what we have learned about the keys to the ministering of angels and the gospel of repentance and baptism. Remember, that it is in part by the ministering of angels that men begin to exercise faith in Jesus Christ (see Moroni 7:25). Faith in Christ is the first principle of the gospel. It motivates and precedes repentance. When God's children obtain faith in Jesus Christ, they are drawn to Him. They begin to desire the peace that comes from having His Spirit to be with them. As angels minister to them and promote faith within them, God's children are drawn to the covenants that eternally bind them to their Savior. They soon find within themselves a desire to be baptized or to partake of the sacrament worthily to earnestly renew their baptismal covenants that they may be (re)united with the Savior.

In considering these first principles and ordinances of the gospel, is it any wonder why the bishop is an Aaronic Priesthood office? He holds the keys to administer the covenants (baptism and sacrament) that allow God's children to receive the ministry of angels. It is the bishop, who as president of the Aaronic Priesthood, represents the Lord in ensuring that repentance is sufficiently sincere and complete to allow for the Atonement to be activated. As you or I work together with a holder of these preparatory keys, the Spirit of the Lord is engaged to fulfill His divinely appointed role to sanctify our repentant souls by offering those sacred feelings of forgiveness and love as we convey our preparation to participate in the ordinances that deliver a remission of our sins.

Mormon elaborated: "Wherefore, by the ministering of angels, and by every word which proceeded forth out of the mouth of God, men began to exercise faith in Christ; and thus by faith, they did lay hold upon every good thing; and thus it was until the coming of Christ. And after that he came men also were saved by faith in his name; and by faith, they become the sons of God" (Moroni 7:25–26).

With the aid of ministering angels speaking the words of the Holy Ghost as well as through the access we have to the words of God, we are able to access the first principle of the gospel. As we exercise faith to respond to the words of the prophets and of the angels, we are drawn toward Christ who prepares us to benefit from the Aaronic Priesthood principle of repentance and its associated ordinances.

In 1998, Dallin H. Oaks spoke about the role of Aaronic Priesthood ordinances and the keys held within that priesthood. He taught these doctrines beautifully as follows:

> What does it mean that the Aaronic Priesthood holds the "key of ministering angels" and of the "gospel of repentance and of baptism and of the remission of sins"? The meaning is found in the ordinance of baptism and the sacrament. Baptism is for the remission of sins, and the sacrament is the renewal of the covenants and blessings of baptism. Both should be preceded by repentance. When we keep the covenants made in these ordinances, we are promised that we will always have his Spirit to be with us. The ministering of angels is one of the manifestations of that Spirit.[1]

Relating this back to the ordinances of the preparatory gospel administered by Aaronic Priesthood holders, I am impressed by the majesty of God's methods. As a repentant soul approaches the ordinance of the sacrament, having prepared themselves for personal angelic ministry, they are qualified to receive the power of the Holy Ghost to convey to them the mercy, empowerment, and healing that the Atonement of Jesus Christ offers them. This happens only as they hear the sacrament prayer as spoken by the priests and receive the sacramental emblems from the deacons. Without these Aaronic Priesthood holders, it would be impossible for the Lord to one by one provide His children with His sacred communion, the symbol of His forgiveness.

A wise judge in Israel will help repentant people be sensitive to feel these angels facilitating a quiet but powerful and deeply personal coming of the Lord into their lives as these sacred ordinances are administered. He will also teach those priests, teachers, and deacons about the reverence required to allow for this sacred communion to occur. He may teach them to watch over his members as they partake of the sacrament so that they might also recognize the full measure of the administration of these sacred Aaronic Priesthood keys.

As God's daughters and sons diligently lean on their faith in Christ, they are allowed access to the healing, enabling, and redeeming power of His Atonement. For members under the covenant of baptism, which you must believe also includes YOU, the path to the healing, enabling, and redemptive power of the Atonement does not have to be a lonely one to be walked alone. The descent to your knees in sincere prayer, the sit-down chat with a parent, or the walk to a bishop's office will always require great courage, but the peace that comes as we seek to repent cannot be matched. Given that the Aaronic Priesthood holds the keys to the gospel of repentance, it is both obvious and essential that those who minister in this priesthood become deeply acquainted with its power. Repentance can be defined in even very simple terms as a gift that allows you and I to seek lasting change in our thoughts and actions that will enable us to receive the overwhelming gift of forgiveness. The peace, hope, and happiness that come with the Lord's mercy can be confirmed when sincere repentance is combined with the Aaronic Priesthood ordinances of baptism and repentance as you and I receive the sacred Aaronic Priesthood ordinances of baptism and the sacrament.

Elder Oaks further outlined the important role of the ordinances of baptism and the sacrament in accomplishing the Lord's purposes to establish peace. As you read his words, pay attention to how the lesser Aaronic Priesthood offices are called upon to support the bishop in his role to administer the gospel of repentance.

> We are commanded to repent of our sins and to come to the Lord with a broken heart and a contrite spirit and partake of the sacrament in compliance with its covenants. When we renew our baptismal covenants in this way, the Lord renews the cleansing effect of our baptism. In this

> way we are made clean and can always have His Spirit to be with us. The importance of this is evident in the Lord's commandment that we partake of the sacrament each week (see Doctrine and Covenants 59:8–9).
>
> *We cannot overstate the importance of the Aaronic Priesthood in this.* All of these vital steps pertaining to the remission of sins are performed through the saving ordinance of baptism and the renewing ordinance of the sacrament. *Both of these ordinances are officiated by holders of the Aaronic Priesthood under the direction of the bishopric, who exercise the keys of the gospel of repentance and of baptism and the remission of sins.*[2]

Elder Oaks continued by teaching further about how these ordinances of the preparatory gospel are tied to the Aaronic Priesthood keys related to the ministering of angels and again identified the role of the lesser offices in exercising this priesthood key.

> How does the Aaronic Priesthood hold the key to the ministering of angels? The answer is the same as for the Spirit of the Lord.
>
> In general, the blessings of spiritual companionship and communication are only available to those who are clean. As explained earlier, through the Aaronic Priesthood ordinances of baptism and the sacrament, we are cleansed of our sins and promised that if we keep our covenants we will always have His Spirit to be with us. I believe that promise not only refers to the Holy Ghost but also to the ministering of angels, for "angels speak by the power of the Holy Ghost; wherefore, they speak the words of Christ" (2 Nephi 32:3). So it is that those who hold the Aaronic Priesthood open the door for all Church members who worthily partake of the sacrament to enjoy the companionship of the Spirit of the Lord and the ministering of angels.[3]

In aligning the role of heavenly angels to call men to repentance with the role of the mortal holders of the Aaronic Priesthood, we see clearly the synchronization of their priesthood functions. As bishops work with deacons, teachers, and priests to be active in their respective roles to do the work of the covenants, the power of the Aaronic Priesthood is harnessed. In so doing, Aaronic Priesthood holders open the door that can allow heavenly angels to fulfill their comparable duty "to call men unto repentance" "by declaring the word of Christ unto the chosen vessels of the Lord that they may bear testimony of him" (Moroni 7:31).

Several years ago, I saw in a very practical way how one thoughtful judge in Israel leveraged one of his Aaronic Priesthood quorums to administer the preparatory gospel and invite his ward members to partake of the gospel of repentance. At that time, I lived in a ward with a large group of priests, and I served as a quorum adviser. Most of the priests were considering, if not already well-preparing, for missionary service. Our bishop at that time recognized not only the need to prepare these young men for Melchizedek Priesthood service but also of the need to allow them to fulfill their own Aaronic Priesthood duties to administer the preparatory gospel in our ward. In our quorum lessons, the bishop taught about the priest's duty "to visit the house of each member, and exhort them to pray vocally and in secret and attend to all family duties" (D&C 20:47).

To assist the bishop in administering the Aaronic Priesthood keys and to fulfill their duty to God, the bishop asked the quorum advisers to work with the priests to help them learn how to minister by preparing lesson plans developed using *Preach My Gospel.* The bishop then worked with the advisers to identify families in the ward who would be receptive to a visit from a companionship of priests. These priests were assigned to visit the family in their home and to share a missionary lesson with them. This proved to be a beautiful experience that strengthened faith throughout the ward.

I remember the first visit that was scheduled. I went to the home of a family in our ward with two sixteen–year-old young men, Andy and Jacob. The two priests knew that they were in charge. We arrived in the home, and the family was quickly gathered. Nervously, Andy sat in silence while Jacob fidgeted with his scriptures for what felt like forever, fumbling to find the verse he had prepared. There was barely a greeting or expression of gratitude extended by the priests. The gracious family waited patiently amid the terrifically uncomfortable silence. It was all that I could do to not bail them out by bridging the conversation with common pleasantries. After a few very long moments, Andy finally stammered, "We have a message we'd like to share." He began reading a verse in the Book of Mormon. Following the scripture, he shared what barely qualified as a testimony, stating that he knew that we can be happy if we follow the words of King Benjamin. He followed it up with the most convincing statement of the visit by exclaiming, "Thank you for letting us come tonight!" As he stood up and beelined it for the door, I could see the sweat dripping down his face as we left the house not even five minutes after having arrived. We had entered the home planning on visiting for fifteen or twenty minutes. Within a mere three hundred seconds it was all over, and the three of us had escaped out the front door.

Our visit had been a complete disaster—and it was fantastic! These boys had felt the real pain of having to talk to somebody with whom they were not well acquainted and to share a message that was only meagerly prepared. In less than five minutes, it felt as if they had done more to prepare for missionary service than could have been accomplished in two years of priesthood lessons. Relieved that the visit was over, the two priests walked quickly to the car, where I excitedly reminded them that we had a second appointment.

We had a wonderful opportunity to review the visit and learn from the experience. These priests began to learn and grow within the safety of our own ward, where they were free from judgment or scorn and where they could become all that the Lord needed them to be both in their current Aaronic Priesthood assignment and as future missionaries.

Over the next several months, the assignment persisted with different families being visited each month. The priests gained confidence and competence with each visit. They learned how to ask questions and how to engage both adults and children. They became familiar with the doctrines of the gospel and developed skills for presenting the *Preach My Gospel* lessons. They practiced testifying with power.

I will never forget the last night I was able to be a part of these visits before being released as their adviser. I listened as two high school seniors filled with the Spirit bore a sincere and powerful testimony and extended invitations for a family to ponder the scriptures and to pray. With power and authority, they fulfilled their priesthood duty to warn, exhort, expound, teach, and invite others to come unto Christ. They left the house and begged to find another family for us to visit. We scrambled and found two more families that night, including a visit to one of their own homes where we were met by surprised parents who were astonished by the power of the Aaronic Priesthood keys being exercised that night.

I have reflected often on how this experience helped these young men prepare for their future Melchizedek Priesthood service. I remember being impressed by the missionary spirit that consumed these young priests as they made time in their busy schedules and looked forward to this monthly assignment from the perceptive and purposeful bishop. I learned, though, that this experience was not just about preparing young men for the Melchizedek Priesthood. This experience was equally about activating the keys of the Aaronic Priesthood in our ward to prepare our ward members—*our* people—for the coming of the Lord.

I saw active ward members who were touched by the sincere and struggling young men. I saw other families whose waning church activity was strengthened as they heard the voice of ministering angels fulfilling their ministry to call them to repentance, whispering to them words of the Holy Ghost. I saw parents of priests gain perspective as they witnessed the Aaronic Priesthood potential being realized as their sons fulfilled their duty to God. The power of the Aaronic Priesthood had been harnessed, and the keys to the ministering of angels and to the gospel of repentance had been activated. I saw a bishop who was sustained in his capacity to administer the gospel of repentance. I like to think that the line outside of his office was just a little bit longer as individuals and families seeking happiness in their life followed promptings they had received to repent during these priesthood visits.

As the priests in our ward exercised their priesthood authority, I am confident that ministering angels attended to the members of our ward, leading them to strengthen their faith in Christ. I am confident that the sacrament became a more powerful influence within our ward because these young men fulfilled their duty to visit the house of each member and to preach and teach and invite individuals and families to seek the Savior. With angels attending, the words of Christ were declared, and testimonies were strengthened sufficient that these chosen vessels of the Lord (both the priests and the ward members) were prepared to bear testimony of Christ.

In a short period of time, mission calls began to arrive for these well-prepared priests who were empowered with the gift of the Holy Ghost and the ability to speak with that power—even as the angels. The Aaronic Priesthood purposes were fulfilled as the young men left to share their witness with "the residue of men that they might have faith in Christ" (Moroni 7:31). Furthermore, the families that stayed behind were strengthened and better acquainted with the Master as they sought to honor their own priesthood covenants.

The keys to the ministry of angels is not complicated. Rather, it is through these seemingly small and simple acts of service and through the administration of preparatory ordinances that the Aaronic Priesthood fulfills its purposes to prepare the way for God's children to meet the Master. While we all look forward to the glorious day when the Lord will come again, the more immediate need is to build our faith in Jesus Christ, to partake of the gospel of repentance, and to make and renew priesthood covenants, that we may sanctify ourselves, that our minds may become more and more single to God. With capable judges in Israel carefully administering Aaronic Priesthood service, the Lord's purposes to bring about the ordinances of salvation to His children will be accomplished, and you as a holder of that priesthood have the great privilege of taking part.

NOTES

1. Dallin H. Oaks, "The Aaronic Priesthood and the Sacrament," churchofjesuschrist.org/study/general-conference/1998/10/the-aaronic-priesthood-and-the-sacrament?lang=eng. Accessed May 26, 2020.
2. Ibid.
3. Ibid.

THE GOSPEL OF REPENTANCE AND BAPTISM

As I Strive to Serve, Exercise Faith, Repent, and Improve Each Day

DOCTRINE

Review the Aaronic Priesthood duties in Doctrine and Covenants 20:53–55; 57–59. Read the entry for "Ministry" in the Bible Dictionary. Look for references that suggest Aaronic Priesthood participation and responsibility in the work of Ministry.

PRINCIPLE

Lead a discussion with your bishop and quorum to evaluate the ways that the duties within each Aaronic Priesthood office support the administration of the gospel of repentance. Be sure to include the office of bishop in your discussion.

Discuss with your bishop and your quorum why ministering is an important aspect of administering the gospel of repentance.

THEORY

Journal your thoughts on ministering. Set goals for how you will fulfill your own personal ministry to deliver the gospel of repentance.

Counsel together with your bishop and quorum presidency to evaluate the current state of Aaronic Priesthood ministering in your ward. Develop an Aaronic Priesthood ministering plan to sustain your bishop in his administration of the keys to the gospel of repentance.

Be thoughtful and creative to consider various ways that your quorum members can minister to the chosen vessels of your ward as you "teach, preach, exhort, and invite them to come unto Christ."

CHAPTER 6

Preparing for Melchizedek Priesthood Power

I Will Qualify to Receive Temple Blessings and the Enduring Joy of the Gospel

---

And the sons of Moses and of Aaron shall be filled with the glory of the Lord, upon Mount Zion in the Lord's house, whose sons are ye; and also many whom I have called and sent forth to build up my church.

—DOCTRINE AND COVENANTS 84:32

When Moses was called to serve as the prophet for the Israelites, he would have certainly felt very overwhelmed. The Israelite people were slaves to the Egyptians, and the assignment fell upon Moses to figure out a way to liberate thousands of people, unite them together, and lead them to a promised land free from bondage. Notwithstanding his divine appointment, Moses was still just a man with the same human frailties that you and I might possess. Seeking confidence and support, he looked to the Lord to send him help. The Lord responded by sending Moses his older brother, Aaron.

Aaron and Moses were separated before they ever knew each other. At the time of Moses's birth, the Egyptian Pharaoh had ordered that all Israelite baby boys be killed. You will remember that to protect her infant son, Moses's mother placed him in a basket and floated him in the river where he could be found and raised by Pharaoh's daughter. Moses was separated not only from his mother but also from the rest of his family, including Aaron, who was just three years older than Moses. Imagine their mother's heartache. She had certainly dreamed of seeing them grow up together, and to protect them she had been compelled to make this courageous choice to separate them.

Moses would go on to earn fame and great respect as a member of Pharaoh's royal court, while Aaron remained with his family, subject to the slavery and oppression imposed by Pharaoh upon the Israelite nation.

Though it would take many years, the two brothers were destined to reunite and become great in the sight of God. Soon after his eightieth birthday, Moses's status before Pharaoh and even his life would be in jeopardy after Moses killed an Egyptian man to preserve the life of one of his Israelite brethren. At this time of great vulnerability, God called Moses to be his prophet and to return to Egypt to rescue the Israelite people.

In his vulnerability, Moses plead with the Lord for help to accomplish this awesome assignment. The Lord responded by calling Aaron to leave his family and go out into the wilderness to meet Moses, who was still in hiding. Imagine Aaron's love and faithfulness. He recognized the call that had come from the Lord. He did not waver in his response. He did not question why the Lord had called Moses, who had never lived as an Israelite, and not someone more like himself, who may have been better acquainted with the Israelite people and their unique needs.

Aaron would soon be called to assist Moses in every way, even being called to speak for Moses, who had difficulty communicating on his own to the people. Through Moses, the Lord would also institute his preparatory priesthood, giving the Israelites access to the covenants and ordinances that would prepare them for the promised land, for their days when they could meet the Messiah.

Aaron was a member of the tribe of Levi. The Levites were assigned to be led by Aaron as they served the children of Israel and provided them with the ordinances that would enable them to become clean and prepared to enter the sanctuary of the Lord. In the earliest of Aaronic Priesthood assignments, their purpose was clearly to prepare the people for the coming of the Messiah by doing the work of the covenant. These preparatory assignments remained with Aaron and these "sons of Levi" for many generations as referenced in this verse from the Old Testament: "And I have given the Levites as a gift to Aaron and to his sons from the among the children of Israel, *to do the service of the children of Israel in the tabernacle of the congregation, and to make an atonement for the children of Israel:* that there be no plague among the children of Israel, when the children of Israel come nigh unto the sanctuary" (Numbers 8:19; emphasis added).

One of assignments of the sons of Levi was to account for the names of all of the children of Israel to ensure that each had received the necessary ordinances of salvation. "And Moses and Aaron took these men which are expressed by their names: And they assembled all the congregation together on the first day of the second month and *they declared their pedigrees after their families,* by the house of their fathers, according to the number of names, from twenty years old and upward, by their polls" (Numbers 1:17–18; emphasis added).

Similarly, the Aaronic Priesthood today prepares people for the coming of the Lord and does the work of the covenants as it administers the gospel of repentance and its associated ordinances that prepare people to make the higher temple covenants and receive the greater ordinances of the Melchizedek Priesthood. As promised to both John the Baptist and to Joseph Smith, it is also true that the Aaronic Priesthood has an important duty that pertains to the spirit of Elijah and the gathering of Israel.

You will recall that when John the Baptist was born it was promised that he would play a key role in the turning of the hearts of the fathers to the children and similarly the hearts of the children to their fathers. You may also recall that complicated language given by John to Joseph Smith when he said that the Aaronic Priesthood "would never again be taken from the earth, until the sons of Levi do offer again an offering unto the Lord in righteousness" (D&C 13:1).

Let's put this all together. We know that Aaron and the sons of Levi had the responsibility of gathering all of the children of Israel, organizing them by name, and preparing them to make covenants and receive ordinances. We know that John the Baptist was sent to turn the hearts of the children to their fathers and that with the restoration of the Aaronic Priesthood, that mandate was again implemented in our day. We also know by experience the potential that today's Aaronic Priesthood holders have to continue in this ancient tradition of organizing family names, "declaring their pedigrees after their families" for the purpose of preparing those individuals who have died to receive the exalting ordinances of the temple. The sons of Levi's offering of righteousness is at least in part a commitment to deliver to the Lord the names of all of His children so that they may receive the ordinances of the temple.

The Lord invites all of the covenanted members of His church to participate in this important Aaronic Priesthood purpose by making our own contributions to this great offering. Check out what He says here about the work He has called us to do in these latter days: "Behold, the great day of the Lord is at hand . . . and he shall purify the sons of Levi, and purge them as gold and silver, that they may offer unto the Lord an offering in righteousness. *Let us, therefore, as a church and a people, and as Latter-Day Saints, offer unto the Lord an offering in righteousness; and let us present in his holy temple, when it is finished, a book containing the records of our dead,* which shall be worthy of all acceptation" (D&C 128:24; emphasis added).

Isn't that cool? The Lord invites all of us—men and women, young women and men, Primary children—to prepare the names of our kindred dead to receive their ordinances in the temple. Can you imagine what the sons of Levi would have thought to see Family Search today? This is such an exciting time to be alive when the fulness of the gospel has been restored and we can be active participants in the work that will enable billions of people to make covenants with God.

As an Aaronic Priesthood holder, a key component of your preparation for Melchizedek Priesthood stewardship and your own temple covenants is to understand the elements of the oath and covenant of the priesthood that will be committed to you when you receive the higher priesthood. The components of this covenant are outlined in the familiar verses found in Doctrine and Covenants 84:31–48 and include the following commitments that you will make as you receive the Melchizedek Priesthood:

- Magnify your calling (see verse 33).
- Give diligent heed to the words of eternal life (see verse 43).
- Live by every word that comes from the mouth of God (see verse 44).

In turn, to all those who honor the covenants made when receiving the higher priesthood, God swears an oath promising the following eternal blessings:

- Sanctified by the Spirit (see verse 33).
- Renewing of their bodies (see verse 33).
- Become the sons of Moses and of Aaron and the seed of Abraham, and the church and kingdom, and the elect of God (see verse 34).
- Receive the Father and all that He has (see verse 38).

Different from saving baptismal and temple ordinances, there is not a formal sign or symbol of the covenant made when the Melchizedek Priesthood is conferred. Rather, we are pointed only to the scriptures to learn of the oath and covenant and ultimately to the temple.

In the temple the culminating Melchizedek Priesthood ordinances are received. It is only in the temple where the full significance of receiving the oath and covenant of the priesthood and all that belongs to the Father can begin to be fully contemplated. As members of gathered Israel, the Lord promises that we shall be filled with the glory of the Lord as we make and keep temple covenants (see Doctrine and Covenants 84:32). As such, your greatest goal during this preparatory part of your life should be to qualify yourself for the blessings of the temple.

It is in the temple where the majestic and indiscriminate power of the priesthood is fully made manifest to both men and women, both equally and jointly, as husband and wife are brought together to be sealed. When placed under covenant, they are promised that together they can receive all that the Father has to give if they keep their covenants. Try comprehending the notion that *all* that the Father has can be given to His sons and daughters through the sealing covenant.

When you receive the Melchizedek Priesthood and are ordained to the office of Elder, you will make the covenants that we already noted in Doctrine and Covenants 84. In giving yourself to the Lord, in a very real way, you will exercise your agency and promise that from that day forward you will "magnify his calling," "to give diligent heed to the words of eternal life," and "live by every word that proceeds from the mouth of God."

You will also covenant to be an earthly minister of Jesus Christ and to fulfill the Lord's objectives. In so doing, you will commit your agency to Jesus Christ and seek to act and serve God's children as the Savior would if He were here. The priesthood holder commits to become a dependable instrument in the hand of the Lord. Because of this, it is no wonder that we define the priesthood as the authority to act in the name of the Lord. As one who has effectively given himself to Christ, your solemn obligation is to now always exercise your agency as if you are acting on behalf of the Savior Himself.

In so giving yourself to God as an ordained Elder, you will exercise your agency to leave behind the choice to follow the world and commit yourself to serve the Father, the only true God, and Jesus Christ. In giving yourself freely and wholly, you will now be committed to do the will of the Lord. You will come to know the will of the Lord as you fulfill the covenants associated with your priesthood ordination. More specifically, you will come to know the will of the Lord as you study to learn the words of eternal life, as you strive to obey every word that comes from God, and as you magnify your purpose and capability by drawing on the enabling power of the Atonement of Jesus Christ to bring God's children unto the Messiah.

With this commitment, you now can qualify for the full blessings of God's power and glory as you fulfill your newfound duty to create a family bound by the sealing power of the priesthood and obtained only in the new and everlasting covenant of marriage.

Elder Bruce R. McConkie taught this truth as follows:

> The Melchizedek Priesthood is the highest and holiest order ever given to men on earth. It is the power and authority to do all that is necessary to save and exalt the children of men. It is the very priesthood

> held by the Lord Jesus Christ himself and by virtue of which he was able to gain eternal life in the kingdom of his Father."
>
> Those who receive the Melchizedek Priesthood, covenant and promise before God, and angels, to magnify their callings, to "live by every word that proceedeth forth from the mouth of God," to marry for time and all eternity in the patriarchal order, and to live and serve as the Lord Jesus did in his life and ministry.[1]

Embedded in this teaching is the admonition that Melchizedek Priesthood holders retain the obligation to seek out and marry for time and all eternity. The blessings of the sealing covenants are worthy of every sacrifice and preparation. That preparation should include learning all that you can about what it means to be sealed and what will be required of you when it is your turn to kneel at an altar in a holy temple.

As the sealing covenant is made, sacred words are spoken that allow both husband and wife the opportunity to agree to "receive" the other. The promises in the sealing ordinance are sacred and beautiful and include a promise to the sealed family that as they keep their covenant, they can qualify themselves for what can be summed up in the familiar phrase—"all that my Father hath" (D&C 84:38).

With that promised blessing in mind, consider how closely tied the sealing ordinance is to the oath and covenant of the priesthood. The oath and covenant outlined in the Doctrine and Covenants promises that those who receive this priesthood can qualify themselves to receive all that the Father has to give. The thought of receiving everything that belongs to Heavenly Father is so magnificent that it is truly beyond our mortal comprehension.

For my simple mind, I like to trust that this gift is everything that could ever bring me joy and happiness that will last through the eternities. The Young Men's theme succinctly defines this promised blessing as "the enduring joy of the gospel." This enduring joy is the promise that you and I can continue to progress forever and that through this eternal progression, we can become like God. In essence, within this promised priesthood covenant is the power to be like Heavenly Father, a power otherwise known as godliness. Remember that it is in the ordinance (think sealing) that the power of godliness is manifest. As we give ourselves to the Lord through our priesthood and temple covenants, we become His possessions, and He can then, by virtue of the sealing ordinance, give us to a deserving spouse and together we can be qualified to become like our Heavenly Parents. With these truths in mind, it becomes obvious why a temple marriage is worthy of your every pursuit.

Take a moment to slow down in your reading to consider the magnificent blessings promised to the newly pronounced husband and wife in the sealing ordinance, which include the bestowal of all things that pertain to becoming an heir to our Heavenly Father's inheritance. In reflecting on those words, read the following verses pertaining to the oath and covenant of the priesthood that provide God's capstone promises given to His sons and daughters who are joined together under the sealing covenant.

> And also all they who receive this priesthood receive me, saith the Lord; For he that receiveth my servants receiveth me; And he that receiveth me receiveth my Father; And he that receiveth my Father receiveth my Father's kingdom; therefore all that my Father hath shall be given unto him. And this is according to the oath and covenant which belongeth to the priesthood. (D&C 84:35–39)

If we really believe that the wide-eyed young man at the altar is a priesthood holder and covenanted servant of the Lord, and that the sincere and beautiful young woman receiving him on the other side of that altar is similarly endowed with power bestowed upon her in the temple, we can find great hope and be ensured that collectively they are qualified to receive the Lord, His Father, His kingdom, and even all that the Father has to give.

Seeing the role of women in accomplishing the Lord's priesthood purposes to seal God's children up to Him gives leagues of depth to some of the often more casually viewed scriptures regarding the value of righteous women. For example, in the New Testament Paul taught, "Neither is the man without the woman, neither the woman without the man, in the Lord" (1 Corinthians 11:11).

Truly the man and woman are equal in the sight of the Lord. The culminating covenants of the priesthood are without effect if only one spouse arrives at the altar. When priesthood power is fully recognized in its requirement for both men and women to be individually present and under covenant for a couple to be sealed up unto the Lord, concerns about gender equality can subside. We see that the roles of man and woman in the sealing covenant are unique unto themselves, but incomplete without the other. We can observe how a righteous man, however faithful, is only eligible for the full glory of the Father when united under priesthood covenant with his wife. Similarly, a righteous wife, however faithful, can only receive the full glory of the Father after receiving her husband from the Lord in a temple sealing.

To understand the full breadth of the preparatory priesthood, it is important that we seek to understand the magnitude of these Melchizedek Priesthood blessings available to both men and women that the Aaronic Priesthood prepares each of us to receive. One of the most beautiful but overlooked elements of a temple sealing is the practical nature of the covenants that are made. In addition to receiving the promised blessings, men and women also covenant to pursue practical applications of the gospel of Jesus Christ to qualify their family for the blessings of the sealing covenant. Specifically, husbands are placed under covenant to preside in their families with the priesthood principles of *gentleness, meekness,* and *love unfeigned.* These same principles are familiar because they are clearly outlined by the Lord as part of His admonition to honor their priesthood covenants. These principles were revealed to Joseph Smith while he sat in the darkness that occupied the Liberty Jail: "No power or influence can or ought to be maintained by virtue of the priesthood, only by persuasion, by long-suffering, by *gentleness* and *meekness,* and *love unfeigned*" (D&C 121:41; emphasis added).

These are practical principles that can be developed now as a preparatory priesthood holder. They are principles of power that will qualify you to one day arrive at an altar, prepared to pursue the power of godliness with someone you love.

It was David of the Old Testament who perhaps most eloquently recognized the power and potential in these practical presiding principles when he praised the gentleness of the Lord: "Thou hast also given me the shield of thy salvation: *and thy gentleness hast made me great*" (2 Samuel 22:36; emphasis added).

David recognized how his greatness came because of the gentleness that the Lord had shown him. It is interesting to parallel this verse of David's psalm with the language in the sealing ordinance that invokes a man to guide his marriage and family with the same gentleness that the Lord uses to administer salvation to His children. Like David, one of the greatest gifts parents can give to their sons is to prepare them for Melchizedek Priesthood service within their families by instilling the practical principles that will allow them to become like David, who was made great by the gentleness of the Lord.

While these principles of gentleness, meekness, and love unfeigned are often best learned by example, it is my experience that by being explicit in connecting examples with instructions, it can be very helpful in ensuring that young men come to value the power that comes with being a true *gentle* man. It is well documented that men sometimes struggle to be openly gentle and meek. Sometimes we tend to reserve our unfeigned, or most sincere love, for only our most private moments. It is imperative that young men work to overcome these natural tendencies by learning to express themselves with tenderness and meekness.

Within the construct of your Aaronic Priesthood quorum, you have a wonderful training ground to learn the elements of unfeigned love, meekness, and gentleness through both explicit instruction and positive experiences in quorum activities. With some effort, your quorum presidency can create opportunities for you and the other members of your quorum to be instructed by one another and to receive a witness of these priesthood principles from the Holy Ghost.

I once saw this play out in a simple but inspiring way on an overnight campout with a group of deacons. Our quorum had a new group of eleven–year-old deacons who were excited but nervous to be part of the quorum and on their first campout.

Our quorum has a wonderful campout tradition that we call "stick on the fire." We gather around a campfire, and each deacon is invited to lay a stick on the fire to burn while they share a spiritual thought, testimony, or even something they enjoyed from the day's activity. As we gathered that night for our campfire, we began with this tradition as usual with our quorum president setting the first stick on the fire and providing a short opening discussion that included some thoughts on what it means to be a gentle man. We laughed together as we discussed the rock band irony of the phrase "Ladies and Gentlemen" that is used at concerts and monster truck rallies—venues that are typically far from gentle. We participated in a discussion about the importance of learning how to be gentle and meek. We also discussed unfeigned love.

One of the focuses of our campfires is to enable a disarming dynamic where we make it clear that it is okay and, more important, even very good to be comfortable discussing things that are tender or of a spiritual nature—especially when outside of church. We strive to create a setting where deacons can be comfortable within this dynamic that is difficult to create just about anywhere else.

On this night, with a little effort and a lot of help from attending angels, we experienced gentleness and were able to identify it as a principle of priesthood power. Within this quiet setting, we had several of these younger deacons step forward and share, some for the first time, simple spiritual experiences that allowed us to recognize these preparatory principles of gentleness, meekness, and love that would enable a newfound unity to be established within the quorum.

One young man shyly stepped forward and placed a small branch of sagebrush on the fire. As the fire burned brightly, he spoke about the bumpy and muddy dirt road we had driven that afternoon on our way back from our hike. He made a heartfelt but fumbling attempt to compare the bumpy road to the path of repentance and the smooth road that lies ahead after partaking of the Atonement of Jesus Christ. His words were not eloquent, but his willingness to experiment to meekly teach his brethren a gospel principle was priceless.

A second young man stepped forward and acknowledged how nervous he was to come into the quorum just a few months prior. He quelled the nervousness felt by all of the new quorum members by publicly conceding his inadequacy and thanking the deacons quorum president for going out of his way to be friendly to him and to help him to feel welcome in the quorum.

Finally, a third young man shared a deeply personal concern he had for his aunt, who was sick with cancer and who was not active in the Church. Between quiet sobs, he expressed gratitude for her recent humility to ask his grandfather for a priesthood blessing. I was especially touched to see one of the other young men meekly pat this tender-hearted deacon on the back in a quiet demonstration of unfeigned love.

In a final effort to be explicit with these young deacons, we sought to reverently acknowledge the presence of the Holy Ghost that attended us that evening. Moreover, we sought to be explicit in recognizing the Christlike priesthood principles that were present. I believe on this quiet night around the crackling of a campfire, each of these young men received a preparation for their greatest priesthood assignment that will hopefully come several years from now when they quietly covenant with a reflective understanding of what it means to preside with gentleness, meekness, and love unfeigned. It is my hope that in their quiet reflection they will remember the tenderness and attentiveness of the Master, whose gentleness will by then have made them, like David, great—both in the sight of God and in the sight of the virtuous woman whom they have taken with them to the House of the Lord. I hope that in some small way, the unity they developed as a quorum through these practical priesthood principles will enable them to establish unity within a family over which they will one day preside.

As you young men are supported in this preparatory phase by thoughtful parents and advisers, you will be well equipped to receive both the blessings and responsibilities that come with receiving the oath and covenant of the Melchizedek Priesthood. Furthermore, you will have accounted for the practical preparation that will allow you to be, like the sons of Levi, "filled with the glory of the Lord, in the Lord's house" (D&C 84:32) as you make covenants that qualify you for exaltation. With a focus on your future, you can be confident that one day you will look back with gratitude and a firm testimony for how the Aaronic Priesthood has prepared you to receive all that the Father has to give.

NOTE

1. Bruce R. McConkie, "The Doctrine of the Priesthood," churchofjesuschrist.org/study/general-conference/1982/04/the-doctrine-of-the-priesthood?lang=eng. Accessed May 26, 2020.

PREPARING FOR MELCHIZEDEK PRIESTHOOD POWER

I Will Qualify to Receive Temple Blessings and the Enduring Joy of the Gospel

---

DOCTRINE

Read Doctrine and Covenants 128:24.
Look to identify why you have an Aaronic Priesthood responsibility to participate in the work of salvation for those who have died.

Read Doctrine and Covenants 84:38.
Look to identify what is available for you to receive through the oath and covenant of the Priesthood.

Read the following scriptures and look to find the value of women in the sight of God:

1 Corinthians 11:11	1 Corinthians 11:7
Proverbs 31:10–11	Jacob 2:28

Read Doctrine and Covenants 121:4.
Look for principles that, when developed, will prepare you to pursue the power of godliness.

PRINCIPLE

Discuss with your family and quorum what you can do to as a quorum to make a contribution to the offering of the sons of Levi by participating in family history work.

Discuss with your family and quorum the essential purpose of women in accomplishing Heavenly Father's plan to give the power of godliness to His children. Consider how virtuous women enable God's glory to be bestowed upon His children through the sealing ordinance.

Lead your family in a discussion to evaluate how the principles of gentleness, meekness, and love unfeigned are manifest within your family. Discuss how these principles strengthen the unity and sealing power in your family.

THEORY

Commit to a personal goal to prepare people who have died to receive temple ordinances.

Journal what you can do to personally prepare yourself to receive the sealing ordinance and what you can do to promote virtue in the world around you.

Journal your thoughts on what you can do to prepare to receive the Melchizedek Priesthood by developing the principles of gentleness, meekness, and love unfeigned in your personal life, family, and quorum.

CHAPTER 7

Fulfilling Your Duty to God

I Will Prepare to Become a Diligent Missionary, Loyal Husband, and Loving Father by Being a True Disciple of Jesus Christ

---

Now let every man learn his duty, and to act in the office in which he is appointed, in all diligence.

—DOCTRINE AND COVENANTS 107:99

Erivaldo was a deeply religious young man living in a small agricultural community in Brazil. His parents and younger sister had been members of the Church of Jesus Christ for just a few months. Erivaldo was a member of an evangelical church where he served in a missionary calling. I will never forget the night we met Erivaldo standing out on the corner in front of his church with a big smile on his face excited to see us—not because he wanted to join the Church but because he wanted to share his church with my companion and me.

Cautiously we accepted his invitation to participate in the evening meeting at his church, but not without first getting him to agree to come to our sacrament meeting on Sunday inside the second floor of a small building that was best known for housing the local gambling hall and lottery on the first level. This night marked the beginning of an exciting few weeks and friendship that I still cherish today. Erivaldo was a sincere seeker of truth. He cautiously accepted our invitation to read the Book of Mormon. He bravely withstood criticism that he received by the pastors at his church. He was patient in his pursuit of Moroni's promise. I will never forget the afternoon when he shared with us that he had received a witness of the truthfulness of the Book of Mormon. He had fasted for two days straight. (I didn't know that was possible.) With fasting and fervent prayer, he had received a witness that he deemed to be undeniable. Soon thereafter, Erivaldo was baptized.

In 2018, I was able to reconnect with Erivaldo in person. How sweet it was to meet him not above the gambling hall but now outside of a beautiful chapel. He still had that same big smile, and we shared a moment of unfeigned love as we embraced. Erivaldo and I are the same age, separated by just a couple of days. Following his baptism, he served a mission to São Paulo, Brazil. He returned home and married a girl who had been baptized during my time as a missionary by another set of Elders who I knew. He still lived in this small little town where he had served as a bishop, high councilor, and now as a counselor in the bishopric to his brother-in-law, who was the bishop. He had a small family with children who had been born in the covenant and were being taught the gospel of Jesus Christ. Erivaldo is all in.

While his baptism changed Erivaldo's life in a magnificent way, what stands out to me is the preparation that occurred prior to him meeting the missionaries. This preparation qualified him first to receive a testimony and to accept the invitation to come unto Christ, then to serve as a diligent missionary himself, and now to stand tall as a loyal husband and loving father. Though he was yet to be a member of the Church, he had sought truth where he could find it and lived his life in a manner that prepared him as a chosen vessel of the Lord. Erivaldo was and is a true disciple of Christ.

When we, like Erivaldo, choose in our early years to be true disciples of Jesus Christ, we cannot begin to imagine the doors that will be opened by our preparation. The Aaronic Priesthood is the preparatory priesthood that will qualify and prepare you for the blessings and duties that will come to you as a qualified holder of the Melchizedek Priesthood.

In the April 2017 priesthood session of general conference, Bishop Gerald Caussé called attention to the inseparable relationship of the Aaronic and Melchizedek Priesthoods and the exemplary relationship between John the Baptist and Jesus Christ:

> Even though they are vested with different missions and authority, the Aaronic Priesthood and the Melchizedek Priesthood are inseparable partners in the work of salvation. They go hand in hand and have great need of each other.
>
> The perfect model of the close relationship that exists between the two priesthoods is found in the interaction between Jesus and John the Baptist. Can one possibly imagine John the Baptist without Jesus? What would the Savior's mission have been like without the preparatory work performed by John?[1]

As the president of the Aaronic Priesthood, your bishop has a unique role to orchestrate the administration of Aaronic Priesthood keys in the ward to ensure that no Aaronic Priesthood holder is left behind. This includes leveraging the divinely appointed power and authority found within each quorum to, as eloquently stated by Bishop Caussé, "participate in the great work of saving souls—both the souls of those young men who hold it and the souls of those they serve."[2]

A bishop is most effective in administering this priesthood power when he knows and understands the responsibilities and capabilities of each priesthood holder and the office to which they are appointed—including his own Aaronic Priesthood office and his duty to watch over the poor.

Among a bishop's many responsibilities is his Aaronic Priesthood role to be a caretaker of the poor and the needy and to be the keeper of the Lord's storehouse. The bishop watches over the temporal welfare of the members of the Church. Moreover, an attentive bishop can find ways to draw on the power bestowed within his Aaronic Priesthood deacons, teachers, and priest quorums to effect his duty to administer in temporal things and in so doing help his Aaronic Priesthood holders to prepare for their future roles as missionaries, husbands, fathers, and true disciples of Jesus Christ.

Doctrine and Covenants 107 further expounds on this sacred trust to administer in temporal things which we often see manifest in the way a bishop cares for the poor: "The office of a bishop is in administering all temporal things; Nevertheless, a high priest, that is, after the order of Melchizedek may be set apart unto the ministering of temporal things, having a knowledge of them by the Spirit of truth" (D&C 107:69, 71).

In considering this sacred trust, we see how the Lord has entrusted His bishops to know and understand the needs of the members of his ward. The Lord does not leave the bishop to minister alone in his appointed office. Notice the key qualifier noted in the scripture that enables the bishop to minister in temporal things—"having a knowledge of them by the Spirit of truth."

In this verse there is a subtle yet powerful acknowledgment of the underlying priesthood keys offered to all bishops to bless those over whom they have stewardship. Reflect for a moment again on the keys to the ministering of angels that form the foundation for all Aaronic Priesthood service.

We can return to the wonderful words of Nephi regarding that power by which the angels speak. That special knowledge that a bishop draws upon in his ministry may often come from the very tongues of angels who speak to him by the power of the Holy Ghost—giving him that knowledge by the Spirit of Truth. From there he may use that knowledge and the power of discernment to help him determine both the true needs of the individuals and families he serves and how to best minister to each of them.

So, where does a bishop turn to access these angels? In a practical world, where does he obtain the information that he needs to be a wise and profitable steward? Certainly, the bishop follows the admonition of Nephi to "feast upon the words of Christ" and "to pray always, and not faint; that ye must not perform any thing unto the Lord save in the first place ye shall pray unto the Father in the name of Christ, that he will consecrate thy performance unto thee, that thy performance may be for the welfare of thy soul" (2 Nephi 32:9).

Furthermore, a bishop familiar with the keys he holds will consider the ordained earthly angels to whom he can turn for information, understanding, and help to carry out his ministry. He will recognize that at his disposal are the very holders of the Aaronic Priesthood over whom he presides.

By elevating Aaronic Priesthood assignments to extend beyond completing familiar priesthood tasks, bishops can enable deacons, teachers, and priests to understand the underlying priesthood duties that will develop discipleship and prepare young men to be the diligent missionaries, loyal husbands, and loving fathers that the Lord needs you to be. In this way Aaronic Priesthood holders can fulfill Bishop Caussé's commendation to "participate in the great work of saving souls-both the souls of those young men who hold it and the souls of those they serve."

When you as an Aaronic Priesthood holder work under the direction of your bishop to participate in the administration of temporal things, you will make great strides to prepare yourself to serve as a missionary, husband, and father. Like your bishop, you can follow the same pattern established by Nephi to develop a practice of prayer and a familiarity with the language of the angels. This language is not usually learned through fantastic experiences where the veil is parted, but most frequently in the administration of what might otherwise be ordinary Aaronic Priesthood service. We can consider a few examples of how Aaronic Priesthood service can be elevated to develop your discipleship and prepare you for future priesthood assignments.

As a priest, you may receive an assignment to administer the sacrament to someone too ill to attend sacrament meeting. You might consider elevating your service to ask the bishop how you might assist in administering to the temporal needs of those you serve. Seeing your initiative and recognizing your role as a ministering angel, your bishop might ask you to assess certain temporal needs that the family may be facing. Something as simple as making sure that those you serve have a ride to a doctor's office or a meal scheduled is a great way for the tongues of the angels to be loosed and for you to increase your capacity to grow in wisdom and favor with God. As you not only administer the sacred emblems of the Atonement but also seek to learn more about why you are there, the Holy Ghost will be able to communicate needs that are not yet known that can help the bishop in his ministry. Your devotion to the Lord will grow through your deliberate efforts to deliver relief to those who are suffering.

An in-tune bishop may look to the deacons quorum by elevating an assignment to gather fast offerings to also include gathering information relating to needs of specific members. Prior to fast Sunday, a focused deacons quorum president might ask the bishop if there are any specific members of concern who might warrant some special attention. The bishop could ensure that the young deacons are carefully instructed to ask specific information related to the welfare of a family. A deacon might fulfill an assignment to ask an elderly widow about support she is receiving from her family and discover information that can help the bishop in his efforts to coordinate ministry to her. Even simple tasks can prompt great inspiration and bring clear knowledge from the Spirit of Truth, even to the tongues of earthly angels.

The elevation of Aaronic Priesthood service can occur in sometimes subtle ways that go almost unrecognized. Here is a simple hypothetical example of how a bishop might help those whom he serves.

Consider a single mom living in a ward with her children. We will call her Linda. Knowing the unique needs of this family, the bishop counseled with an elders quorum president to recommend that the teachers quorum president be assigned to accompany a faithful and experienced elder to minister to this family. When first approving the ministering assignment, the bishop noted that the assigned Aaronic Priesthood holder would be working under Aaronic Priesthood keys that included his own responsibility to watch over the Church. He commented further on how the Lord's plan for priesthood service perfectly synchronizes Aaronic and Melchizedek Priesthood stewardships to work in concert with one another to accomplish his purposes. Concluding their discussion, he invited the senior Melchizedek Priesthood companion to encourage the activation of Aaronic Priesthood keys in the ministering assignment that was to be given. The bishop then asked the ministering companionship to gain the confidence of the family by faithfully visiting them each month and by looking to identify both temporal and spiritual needs that should be brought to his attention.

In addition to carefully guiding the ministers, the bishop also asked the deacons quorum president to take an extra minute each month when collecting fast offerings at the family's home to ask Linda if there were any projects around the house or other needs that might require some extra help.

As the snow melted the following winter, the assigned ministers learned that there were some projects in the yard that would prove a lot for this mother to manage on her own. They learned that some sprinklers had been broken over the winter and that there were several areas in the yard that were overgrown with weeds where Linda wanted to till and replace with stones to keep the weeds manageable.

Recognizing that this would mean quite a bit of work, the Melchizedek Priesthood companion asked how his Aaronic Priesthood companion thought that they could help the family. The teachers quorum president recognized an opportunity to exercise the keys he held to direct the work of his quorum to fulfill their duty to "watch over the church always, and be with and strengthen them" and "to be a standing minister unto the church" (D&C 84:111). Together they planned to report to the bishop of this sister's need so that it could be discussed in the next ward council meeting.

In tune with the Spirit from his consistent commitment to consult regularly with the Lord, the bishop evaluated the message from his quorum president. He weighed lightening the burden of the family against his desire to not impose on the sister's desire to be self-reliant. In the familiar tongue of the angels, the Holy Ghost confirmed to him the need and a plan for action.

On a Wednesday evening just a few weeks later, that same teachers quorum president, together with his counselors and with the support of Young Men advisers, stood in the yard behind a wheelbarrow and organized a swarming youth group consisting of deacons, teachers, and priests as well as a good number of young women. Within a couple of hours, the weeds were eradicated and replaced by the large pile of rocks that had just disappeared from the driveway. A fresh layer of mulch had also been spread throughout all the flower beds.

The following Sunday in ward council, it was simply reported that Linda greatly appreciated the service that was rendered on her behalf and that it was great to have so many of the youth involved in the service project. Practically speaking, nothing more had occurred, nor needed to be reported.

However, the insightful bishop recognized that there was much more to be acknowledged. The bishop then proclaimed that a miracle had taken place and took the opportunity to help the ward council see the service from his perspective as president of the Aaronic Priesthood. He had observed the keys of the ministry of angels and the gospel of repentance and baptism in action. He had been a witness to the power of priesthood keys in a fifteen-year-old boy who had fulfilled his duty to watch over the Church and to report on the temporal needs in the ward. The bishop had heard the words of the Holy Ghost conveyed by the freckle-faced angel in whom he trusted. He had felt the love that comes from young men and young women bound by a baptismal covenant to "bear one another's burdens, that they may be light" (Mosiah 18:8).

The bishop may have acknowledged further that together they had participated in that great work of saving souls—both the souls of those young men and young women who hold or respectively sustain the Aaronic Priesthood and the souls of those they serve. The bishop bore a powerful testimony that the seemingly ordinary service project was a glorious example of the power of the Aaronic Priesthood to prepare the way for many ward members, even the chosen vessels of the Lord, to experience the charitable words of Christ, to have faith in Him, and to allow the Holy Ghost to enter their hearts; and that collectively they had harnessed the power of the Aaronic Priesthood to do what was "expedient" to the Lord.

Doing what is expedient to the Lord is the essence of effective Aaronic Priesthood service. As Aaronic Priesthood presidencies seek to accommodate what is expedient, they will find preparatory purpose in their service which extends beyond administering in temporal welfare and into all facets of Aaronic Priesthood service.

I remember seeing this once when our newly called bishop took a mildly courageous action to elevate the Aaronic Priesthood within our ward by breaking from a long-established tradition relating to the format for baptisms. Our visionary bishop had prepared the priests in our ward by teaching them about the keys to the gospel of repentance and baptism and the role they had to "do the 'work' of the covenants" (Moroni 7:31) when he called for them to serve as witnesses for all baptisms that occurred in our ward.

I remember the mild uproar that occurred as parents of those preparing for baptism were informed that the tradition of having grandfathers and uncles stand at baptisms as witnesses was coming to an end. Our great bishop took the time in baptismal interviews to teach families that our ward had been blessed with Aaronic Priesthood holders who were equally up to the task to stand as baptismal witnesses. This break from tradition caused some consternation, but I cannot overstate how sweet it was to arrive at my own daughter's baptismal service to see both the young men and young women in our ward fulfilling various assignments at the service, including leading the music, standing as ushers, and most important, seeing those humble priests standing tall on either side of the font doing the work of the covenant as the outward ordinance of baptism was performed for our daughter. I remember feeling so thankful that day for their worthiness to ensure that my child was properly welcomed into the kingdom of God through baptism. As I reflected further on the experience, I understood clearly our bishop's vision. I saw how the bishop was harnessing the power of the Aaronic Priesthood to do what on that day was expedient unto the Lord. I considered the preparation this experience had facilitated that would allow them to lead baptismal services in the far corners of the world as diligent missionaries in the not-too-distant future. I saw how our family and ward literally participated in that great work of saving souls—both the souls of those young men who held the Aaronic Priesthood and the soul of my daughter whom on that day they served.

In a different ward, while serving as a deacons quorum adviser, I was approached by an older brother in our ward who saw a similar opportunity for our deacons to participate in the work of the covenants. This brother held the calling of overseeing the logistical details of coordinating all of the baptisms each month in our stake. It was his job to see that clothing was washed and ready and that rooms were prepared with chairs to accommodate multiple baptisms on the first Saturday of each month. It was furthermore beautiful to see the recent revelatory directives that have allowed for not only priests, but also all baptized members to act under these same Aaronic Priesthood keys, held by a bishop, to participate in this same work of the covenant by serving as witnesses at baptismal services.

Recognizing that setting up chairs throughout the stake center was a bit of a heavy load for a person of his age to tackle alone, he sought the help of the deacons quorum. Feeling like we were tasked with one more assignment, I somewhat begrudgingly accepted the role to support our quorum in gathering together on the Friday before each scheduled baptism to help set up the chairs. In my murmuring, I was soon corrected after the assigned brother asked to visit our quorum to thank the boys for their service. I was humbled when I recognized that this was not just another assignment to the young men, but that this was a wonderful way that they could participate in the work of salvation. I soon changed my entire approach to the assignment and worked to help our quorum president understand and teach the other quorum members how the assignment carried with it the fulfillment of an underlying duty to participate in the work of salvation by exercising their Aaronic Priesthood keys. Instead of complaining, I came to thank the brother for elevating my perspective on what was otherwise a somewhat mundane assignment. He had shown me what it meant for an Aaronic Priesthood holder to do the work of the covenants as the deacons worked together to enable the Lord to reverently make covenants with a few of His precious children.

When priesthood assignments seem to mount, it is important to maintain perspective. The preparation for difficult priesthood assignments begins as sometimes seemingly unimportant tasks are accomplished. It is through these simple assignments that priesthood perspective is developed. The Lord needs a powerful priesthood, and there is no time like the present to prepare Aaronic Priesthood holders for the tall tasks that you will be given in your roles as you grow and mature in your service and qualify yourselves for future priesthood responsibilities as missionaries, husbands, and fathers.

In October 2007, President Henry B. Eyring spoke of the sense of uncertainty and inadequacy that can accompany Aaronic Priesthood holders as you work to process all that is asked of you. He directed his remarks to any boy somewhere in the world that night, perhaps someone even like you, who "is wondering if he can do what being a priesthood holder will require of him."[4]

President Eyring offered a sermon's worth of reassurance which included this sacred promise that can sustain each of us in our respective priesthood assignments:

> So, to the new deacons: remember. He has always taken care of you from your childhood. To the new quorum presidents: remember. To you fathers with children who are a challenge to you: remember, and have no fear. What is impossible for you is possible with God's help in His service. And even when you were very small and in the years since, He has with His power and His Spirit gone before your face and been on your left hand and on your right hand when you went in His service (see Doctrine and Covenants 84:88). You can receive assurance that God will watch over you if you pray for it in faith. I know that.[5]

You can prepare now to be a diligent missionary, husband, and father. You can do this as you challenge yourself to follow the Savior, to be a true disciple of Jesus Christ. True disciples step up when called upon and are attentive to needs that require no call at all. They find purpose in their service and seek the Holy Ghost. They recognize and know deeply that they are engaged in the work of the Lord. True disciples do not fear the unknown but instead are filled with faith. As President Eyring promised, you can receive assurances now that God is with you. He needs you and loves you for all that you are doing to be a true disciple of His Son. In time, your commitment to discipleship will prepare you well to be a diligent missionary, loyal husband, and loving father.

NOTES

1. Gérald Caussé, "Prepare the Way," churchofjesuschrist.org/study/general-conference/2017/04/prepare-the-way?lang=eng. Accessed May 26, 2020.
2. Ibid.
3. Ibid.
4. Henry B. Eyring, "God Helps the Faithful Priesthood Holder," churchofjesuschrist.org/study/general-conference/2007/10/god-helps-the-faithful-priesthood-holder?lang=eng. Accessed May 26, 2020.
5. Ibid.

FULFILLING YOUR DUTY TO GOD

I Will Prepare to Become a Diligent Missionary, Loyal Husband, and Loving Father by Being a True Disciple of Jesus Christ

---

DOCTRINE

Read Doctrine and Covenants 84:88
Look to understand how angels might bear you up in your priesthood service.

Read 2 Nephi 32:2–3, 9.
Look for the patterns and habits that will qualify you to have your service consecrated by Christ

PRINCIPLE

Lead a discussion with your bishopric and quorum about the ways Aaronic Priesthood service can sustain the bishop in his assignment to oversee the work of the covenants and administer in temporal things.

Discuss with your quorum specific ways in which Aaronic Priesthood service can help you to become a true disciple of Jesus Christ and prepare you to become a diligent missionary, loyal husband, and loving father.

THEORY

Commit with your quorum one way that you will elevate your quorum's priesthood service to develop discipleship by fulfilling basic assignments as the Savior would.

In your journal, make a list of commitments you can make to develop discipleship and qualify yourself for the tongue of angels (Holy Ghost) in your priesthood service.

CHAPTER 8

Building on Pillars of Priesthood Power

I Will Help Prepare the World for the Savior's Return by Inviting All to Come unto Christ and Receive the Blessings of His Atonement

---

For God has not given us the spirit of fear; but of power and of love, and of a sound mind.

—2 TIMOTHY 1:7

The evening of December 17, 2010, was like any other holiday night in December at the historic Provo Tabernacle where holiday performers gathered for a rehearsal. Unbeknownst to the performers, a single stage light had been removed from the ceiling to make room for a truss that was to suspend a bank of temporary stage lights to be used for the evening's performance. The light that had been removed was placed on a wooden speaker box inside the attic and was inadvertently left still connected to the building's electricity. As the stage lights went on for the rehearsal, the speaker box in the attic began to warm as the neglected stage light quietly burned brightly inside the dark attic. Within thirty minutes, the speaker box had caught fire, and within hours, the nearly 150–year-old structure was ablaze.

By the next morning, all that stood was the brick shell of the once proud building. For the better part of a year, the building sat while people questioned what would become of the feeble brick façade. Then, nearly ten months later, President Thomas S. Monson stood in general conference and declared that the beautiful structure would be rebuilt and repurposed—this time as a temple of the Lord.

Innovative engineers labored with precision to ensure that the damaged structure could be preserved. In order to prepare the fragile façade for its new priesthood purpose, the structure was braced with a sturdy scaffolding that would prepare the building to be lifted onto permanent pillars that penetrated deep into the earth. These pillars serve as a firm foundation upon which the powerful structure now stands strong to accomplish its prophetic purpose of establishing covenants for generations of God's children.

Like the foundational pillars of the tabernacle turned temple, on May 15, 1829, the immortal words spoken by John the Baptist to Joseph Smith and Oliver Cowdery similarly set the footings for the foundation of priesthood power to be established. With the words, "Upon you my fellow servants," John established pillars of priesthood power to deliver the captives, strengthen the feeble knees, and to lift the hands that would hang down in this dispensation. In so doing, the heavenly visitor also erected a supportive scaffolding that would allow generations of Aaronic priesthood holders to learn, act, and share as they establish a pattern of priesthood service on the eternal priesthood pillars of personal righteousness, love, and knowledge.

This pattern of priesthood service was set anciently and articulated well by the Apostle Paul, another powerful priesthood holder who bestowed three pillars of priesthood power upon his own "son in the faith," Timothy. The Bible Dictionary suggests that Timothy was "perhaps Paul's most trusted and capable assistant." At the time Paul placed his hands upon Timothy's head, he offered him these profound priesthood principles to bless the ministry of his fellow servant as follows: "Wherefore I put thee in remembrance that thou stir up the gift of God, which is in thee by the putting on of my hands. For God hast not given us the spirit of fear; but of *power* and of *love,* and of *a sound mind.* Be not therefore ashamed of the testimony of our Lord, nor of me his prisoner: but be thou a partaker of the afflictions of the gospel according to the power of God" (2 Timothy 1:7–8; emphasis added).

As he conveyed this priesthood calling, Paul carefully identified three pillars of priesthood power, noting that instead of the spirit of fear, God gives the spirit of power, of love, and of a sound mind.

To help you in your quest to both fulfill your preparatory duties within your Aaronic Priesthood office and in your preparation for Melchizedek Priesthood service, it can be helpful for you come to understand and value each of these pillars and their role to enable and sustain true priesthood power. In examining each of these pillars individually, you can come to value what will be required of you as a fellow partaker of the "afflictions of the gospel" and a "fellow servant" of Jesus Christ.

Priesthood Pillar #1—Power (Personal Righteousness)

While Paul does not specifically cite the words "personal worthiness" in the blessing given to Timothy, I think you will agree that upon closer inspection we can clearly see how the "power" that Paul speaks of is, in fact, closely aligned with what we today identify as personal righteousness or worthiness.

Doctrine and Covenants 121 teaches that priesthood power is directly tied to personal righteousness. In this wonderful revelation, the Lord establishes binding links between personal righteousness and priesthood power. In the well-known verse 36, the connection is clear: "That the *rights of the priesthood are inseparably connected with the powers of heaven, and that the powers of heaven cannot be controlled nor handled only upon the principles of righteousness.* That they may be conferred upon us, it is true; but when we undertake to cover our sins, or to gratify our pride, our vain ambition, or to exercise control or dominion or compulsion upon the souls of the children of men, in any degree of unrighteousness, behold, the heavens withdraw themselves; the Spirit of the Lord is grieved; and when it is withdrawn, Amen to the priesthood or the authority of that man" (D&C 121:36; emphasis added).

The Lord is very clear in articulating that personal righteousness preempts priesthood power. The rights of the priesthood are clearly only controlled and handled upon the principles of righteousness. Personal worthiness is a prerequisite for those assigned to prepare the world for the Savior's return. You will be so much more effective in your efforts to invite others to come unto Christ and receive the blessings of the Atonement if you have first qualified yourself for priesthood power by establishing your own firm pillar of personal righteousness.

President Gordon B. Hinckley spoke plainly to Aaronic Priesthood holders on this topic:

> And so, to you young men who hold the Aaronic Priesthood, you have had conferred upon you that power which holds the keys to the ministering of angels. Think of that for a minute.
>
> You cannot afford to do anything that would place a curtain between you and the ministering of angels in your behalf.
>
> You cannot be immoral in any sense. You cannot be dishonest. You cannot cheat or lie. You cannot take the name of God in vain or use filthy language and still have the right to the ministering of angels.
>
> I do not want you to be self-righteous. I want you to be manly, to be vibrant and strong and happy. To those who are athletically inclined, I want you to be good athletes and strive to become champions. But in doing so, you do not have to indulge in unseemly behavior or profane or filthy language.
>
> To you young men who look forward to going on missions, please do not cloud your lives with anything that would cast a doubt upon your worthiness to go forth as servants of the living God.
>
> You must not, you cannot under any circumstances compromise the divine power which you carry with you as ordained ministers of the gospel.[1]

Further illustrating the binding link between personal righteousness and priesthood power is this statement from Elder Jeffrey R. Holland: "But, young men, you will learn if you have not already, that in frightening, even perilous moments, your faith and your priesthood will demand the very best of you and the best you can call down from heaven. You Aaronic Priesthood boys will not use your priesthood in exactly the same way an ordained elder uses the Melchizedek, but all priesthood bearers must be instruments in the hand of God, and to be so, you must be ready and clean, worthy to act."[2]

I remember my own first experience exercising Melchizedek Priesthood power. I felt deeply humbled and reflective on my own preparatory priesthood experience that had taught me the simple truth that an opportunity to exercise the priesthood is an opportunity to act in the name of Jesus Christ. My experience was not one of a great magnitude in its miracle nor perilous in its circumstance. But for me it was poignant in its portrayal of the importance of personal worthiness and its demand of the very best of what my young faith could call down from heaven.

As a newly minted freshman in college, the phone in our apartment rang in the middle of the night in early September. The voice on the other line was a young woman whom I had met just a couple of weeks before and who had become a friend. She said that she was sick and asked quietly if I could awaken one of my roommates so that we could go to her apartment to provide a priesthood blessing. I had been ordained an elder for only about a month. Humbled and feeling the weight of the trust that Heavenly Father had placed in me to be prepared to bless His children through His priesthood, I quietly agreed to go quickly. As I hung up the phone, I remember quietly dropping to my knees in prayer and feeling the weight of my priesthood responsibility wash over me. I prayed that on this night, I could be a worthy vessel for God's power. I thanked my Heavenly Father for trusting me with this opportunity to represent His Son. I contemplated my own personal worthiness and the simple description that I knew of priesthood power to be the authority to act in the literal stead of Jesus Christ. I awoke my roommate, and we knelt together and prayed that we might be granted a portion of the Lord's spirit to deliver with dignity the Lord's intended blessing on that night.

My experience did not deliver a life-saving miracle, but it embedded within me a sense of the magnitude of my ordained responsibility to administer God's power and blessings to His children. That night, as I exercised that holy authority, there was no question in my mind of the Lord's need for His priesthood holders to be, as President Holland admonished, "ready and clean, worthy to act."

Priesthood Pillar #2—Love

In all our Father in Heaven's earthly visits in which He is accompanied by the Savior, His patriarchal introduction includes the pronouncement of His divine love for His only begotten Son. He utters the familiar phrase, "This is my *beloved* Son, in whom I am well pleased." In His own divine priesthood ministry, God, our Father, leaves no doubt of the eternal love of Christ that is required to sustain His power.

The pattern of love is conveyed perhaps more than any other principle throughout the scriptures. It is easy to see how only a perfect love could justify God sacrificing His only son for the salvation of all mankind. The scriptural discourses on charity communicate clearly how only Christlike love, "the greatest of all" (Moroni 7:46), can sufficiently motivate men and women to offer sufficient sacrifice to access the priesthood power that will lead them to salvation and exaltation through Christ's Atonement. Charity, the greatest of these, is a pillar of priesthood power.

God's love is what motivates and enables the most sacred of priesthood services. The love between a man and a woman is sealed in temples by priesthood power founded upon God's love. That sealing priesthood power enables a love that is so powerful it has the capability to bind families together eternally—even transcending death. God's love is also the underlying power that enables healing through Christ's Atonement. Anyone who has felt the song of redeeming love knows that the charity that comes through the Savior is sufficient to heal every wound. When considering how love is the embodiment of these most sacred and even exalting priesthood services, it is easy to declare with great joy that the very essence of priesthood power is love. The pure love of Jesus Christ embodied through priesthood service is the fundamental pillar of priesthood power.

The *Preach My Gospel* manual eloquently explains the role of love as a pillar of priesthood power:

> A man once asked Jesus, "Which is the great commandment in the law?" Jesus replied: "Thou shalt love the Lord thy God with all thy heart, and with all thy soul, and with all thy mind. This is the first and

> great commandment. And the second is like unto it, Thou shalt love thy neighbor as thyself" (Matthew 22:36–39).
>
> "Charity is the pure love of Christ" (Moroni 7:47). It includes God's eternal love for all His children. We are to seek to develop that kind of love. When you are filled with charity, you obey God's commandment and do all you can to serve others and help them receive the restored gospel.
>
> Charity is a gift from God. The prophet Mormon said that we should pray unto the Father with all the energy of heart, that (we) may be filled with this love. (Moroni 7:48). As you follow this counsel and strive to do righteous works, your love for all people will increase, especially those among whom you labor. You will come to feel a sincere concern for the eternal welfare and happiness of other people. You will see them as children of God with the potential of becoming like our heavenly Father, and you will labor in their behalf. You will avoid negative feelings such as anger, envy, lust, or covetousness. You will try to understand them and their points of view. You will be patient with them and try to help them and their points of view. You will be patient with them and try to help them when they are struggling or discouraged. Charity, like faith, leads to action. You will develop charity as you look for opportunities to serve others and give of yourself."[3]

When seeking to understand the components of the love that defines priesthood power, we can turn again to the revelations received by Joseph Smith regarding the oath and covenant of the priesthood. Similar to his requirement for personal righteousness, in these familiar verses the Lord is also clear in explaining that the priesthood has no power nor authority if not first established with love as its underlying foundation, motivator, and purpose: "No power or influence ought to be maintained by virtue of the priesthood, only by persuasion, by long-suffering, by gentleness and meekness, and by love unfeigned; by kindness, and pure knowledge, which shall greatly enlarge the soul without hypocrisy, and without guile- Reproving betimes with sharpness, when moved upon by the Holy Ghost; and then showing forth afterwards and increase of love towards him whom thou has reproved, lest he esteem thee to be his enemy" (D&C 121:41–43).

Consider each of the words that the Lord chose as prerequisites for priesthood power and how they define or embody an aspect of what can be termed as priesthood love: long-suffering, gentleness, meekness, love unfeigned, kindness, pure knowledge, without guile, sharpness, and an increase of love. Remember again that it is gentleness, meekness, and love unfeigned that enable love that is sufficient to seal God's sons to His daughters in holy temples. With this understanding, it becomes even more essential for you, our young Aaronic Priesthood holders, to develop these defining attributes so that you are prepared for the covenants that represent the Savior's ultimate manifestation of priesthood love. As Aaronic Priesthood holders, it is your duty and obligation to put off the natural man to develop these attributes of priesthood love within your quorum.

After a campout that included a new young man who had just moved into our ward, I observed a couple of Aaronic Priesthood holders exchanging less than kind words about the new Aaronic Priesthood holder. The exchange basically amounted to their conclusion that the new deacon "seemed just like a rich kid who is spoiled with everything he has ever wanted."

While disappointed, I recognized that our quorum members had some uncertainty about letting a new, unfamiliar face enter into their group. Teaching the doctrine of charity and the commandment to "pray unto the Father to be filled with this love" (Moroni 7:48) proved to be solid counsel that allowed the two deacons to reflect on their Aaronic Priesthood duty to love their quorum member. I watched over time as they learned to set aside their preconceived notions and to become acquainted with the new young man as they employed gentleness, meekness, and unfeigned love. By allowing them to recognize the love that could be experienced within their quorum, these deacons acknowledged and embraced this pillar of priesthood power.

It was again Paul who taught Timothy: "Let no man despise thy youth; but be thou an example of the believers, in word, in conversation, in charity, in spirit, in faith, in purity" (Timothy 4:12).

Like Paul, we too can despise not the youth of our Aaronic Priesthood holders, but rather teach each other to be examples of the believers in all things, but particularly in love for those we serve.

Priesthood Pillar #3—Knowledge

In receiving the oath and covenant of the priesthood as outlined in Doctrine and Covenants 84, the Lord asks us to covenant with him to "live by *every* word that proceedeth forth from the mouth of God." "Every word" implies that we have a deep knowledge of God's commandments. We can only be obedient as far as we know and understand the commandments of God. To this end, we must study the words of the prophets to obtain knowledge, or to know the word of God.

Dovetailing elegantly with this covenanted expectation to know the words of God are the instructions given to Nephi that tie back to the Aaronic Priesthood keys of the ministering of angels. Nephi taught how he can access the ministering of angels by feasting on the words of Christ: "Angels speak by the power of the Holy Ghost; wherefore, they speak the words of Christ. Wherefore, I said unto you, *feast upon the words of Christ; for behold the words of Christ will tell you all things what ye should do*" (2 Nephi 32:3; emphasis added).

The reference to the tongues of angels in this verse is powerful to me in that it alludes to the Aaronic Priesthood keys of the ministering of angels that can open the door for God's children to receive revelation from the Holy Ghost. Remember that it is the office of the ministry of angels to call men unto repentance. It is the office of the ministry of angels to point God's children to Aaronic Priesthood authority and ordinances to discover redemption and salvation. As all of God's children feast upon the words of Christ, they literally invite angels to come and by the power of the Holy Ghost tell them all things that they should do to partake of Christ's atonement.

In a beautiful, though understated way, the Lord demonstrates how a "sound mind," filled with knowledge obtained by feasting upon the words of Christ, both precedes and stands as a pillar of priesthood power.

Preach My Gospel provides specific clarity that can inspire you and your quorum to work together to obtain spiritual knowledge: "The Lord has said, 'Seek not to declare my word, but first seek to obtain my word, and then shall your tongue be loosed; then, if you desire, you shall have my Spirit and my word, yea the power of God unto the convincing of men' (D&C 11:21). To teach effectively, you need to obtain spiritual knowledge. For you to grow in the gospel and stay on the path that leads to eternal life, you need to develop a habit of gospel study."[4]

A quorum can work together to help each other discover how understanding doctrine is essential in establishing the important priesthood pillar of knowledge. I am familiar with one quorum that sought to follow the pattern set forth in *Preach My Gospel* to study important gospel topics with an activity that they called Deacons and Doctrine.

One Sunday each month, this quorum gathered together at an adviser's home where they brought scriptures and a notebook that had been provided to them. After indulging in some homemade cinnamon rolls, this quorum followed patterns for studying that were established in *Preach My Gospel* to learn the doctrines of the gospel of Jesus Christ.

In addition to studying doctrines together, advisers tried to incorporate different strategies for supporting the quorum presidency in their responsibility to lead. For example, on some occasions, the quorum presidency sat at the head of the table, where they modeled a true priesthood counsel as they led some of the gospel study sessions. As they studied various doctrines, each deacon was given a relevant passage to study with an assignment to look for either a truth or a question related to our doctrinal topic for the day. They were taught to write down their questions and the truths as preparation for sharing what they learned with the quorum.

This doctrinal study was often simple, but it was always impressive to hear the questions that were asked by sincere twelve- and thirteen–year-olds. It was touching to watch them learn how to share a doctrinal truth from the scriptures with their peers. Finally, it was powerful to feel their germinating testimonies as they bore their elementary witness of the truths that we studied.

Frequently I sat with these young giants and could see them in my mind's eye years later building on these practices and principles to invite others to come unto the Savior as full-time missionaries honoring their Melchizedek Priesthood covenant to "obey every word which proceedeth from the mouth of God." I regularly experienced firsthand the preparatory nature of their priesthood service preparing me for my own sabbath-day encounter with the Lord.

When you, as deacons, teachers, and priests gather together as quorums, you stand tall on the foundational pillar of gospel knowledge. You grow in your familiarity with each word that comes from the mouth of God. You will become resolute in your commitment to be a powerful priesthood holder.

The Savior Himself certainly stood tall on His own foundation of priesthood power: "And Jesus increased in wisdom and stature, in favour with God and man" (Luke 2:52).

This simple verse provides a beautiful template for you as a young man to follow in your work to establish your own firm footing supported by your own pillars of priesthood power. Like the Savior, you will grow in stature and will need to be strong and able to carry the "afflictions" of the gospel. You will also be expected to increase in wisdom—both temporally and spiritually. Finally, you too will be required to increase in favor with both God and man.

Like the Provo City Center Temple, as an Aaronic Priesthood holder, you will be dependent on a strong and capable scaffolding to support you while you discover and establish your own foundation built on these three pillars of priesthood power. A strong and supportive scaffolding should be available to every Aaronic Priesthood holder in the form of capable parents, leaders, and a quorum helping him to stand tall and firm. Established on the pillars of power, love, and a sound mind, an Aaronic Priesthood holder is equipped to harness true priesthood power.

John the Baptist's words "Upon you my fellow servants, in the name of Messiah" ring true today. Each Aaronic Priesthood holder is, in fact, a fellow servant with John the Baptist—a servant of Jesus Christ, who in the name of the Messiah is needed to stand tall on pillars of priesthood power. Like the temple, over time the scaffolding that supports you will be removed piece by piece. As you advance to become holders of the higher priesthood, you, like the completed temple, will one day stand ready to deliver the captives, strengthen the feeble knees, and lift the hands that hang down. Firm on this foundation, you will stand ready to participate in and administer the ordinances of exaltation. Upon these pillars of priesthood power, you will take your place as a fellow servant helping to prepare the world for the Savior's return by inviting all to come unto Christ to receive the blessings of His Atonement.

NOTES

1. Gordon B. Hinckley, "Personal Worthiness to Exercise the Priesthood," churchofjesuschrist.org/study/general-conference/2002/04/personal-worthiness-to-exercise-the-priesthood?lang=eng. Accessed May 26, 2020.
2. Jeffrey R. Holland, "Sanctify Yourselves," churchofjesuschrist.org/study/general-conference/2000/10/sanctify-yourselves?lang=eng. Accessed May 26, 2020.
3. *Preach My Gospel: A Guide to Missionary Service* (2004), chapter 6.
4. Ibid., 18.

BUILDING ON PILLARS OF PRIESTHOOD POWER

I Will Help Prepare the World for the Savior's Return by Inviting All to Come unto Christ and Receive the Blessings of His Atonement

---

DOCTRINE

Read 2 Timothy 1:7–8.

- Look for the three pillars of priesthood power—knowledge, love, and a sound mind.
- Look for Paul's invitation to not be ashamed of a testimony and to partake of the affliction of the gospel.

PRINCIPLE

Discuss the following with members of your family or quorum:

- The significance of each pillar of priesthood power identified by Paul.
- What it means to not be ashamed of the testimony of our Lord.
- What it means to be a partaker of the "afflictions" of the gospel.

THEORY

Journal your commitment to live by "every word" that proceeds from the mouth of God as you do the following:

- Repent or change to pursue your own "power" of personal righteousness.
- Develop and show unfeigned "love" for your family and quorum members.

- Develop a "sound mind" committed to understanding doctrine.

With your quorum presidency, develop a plan for your quorum to learn together how to study and understand gospel doctrines; Look to find ways to share what you learn with others along with a specific invitation to come unto Christ

CHAPTER 9

Sons and Daughters of Heavenly Parents

I Will Help Prepare the People for the Coming of the Lord

I am a beloved son of God, and He has a work for me to do.

With all my heart, might, mind, and strength, I will love God, keep my covenants, and use His priesthood to serve others, beginning in my own home.

As I strive to serve, exercise faith, repent, and improve each day, I will qualify to receive temple blessings and the enduring joy of the gospel.

I will prepare to become a diligent missionary, loyal husband, and loving father by being a true disciple of Jesus Christ.

I will help prepare the world for the Savior's return by inviting all to come unto Christ and receive the blessings of His Atonement.

—AARONIC PRIESTHOOD THEME FOR YOUNG MEN

**I am a beloved daughter of Heavenly Parents,
with a divine nature and eternal destiny.**

**As a disciple of Jesus Christ, I strive to become like Him.
I seek and act upon personal revelation
and minister to others in His holy name.**

**I will stand as a witness of God at all times
and in all things and in all places.**

**As I strive to qualify for exaltation, I cherish the gift of
repentance and seek to improve each day. With faith,
I will strengthen my home and family, make and
keep sacred covenants, and receive the ordinances
and blessings of the holy temple.**

–YOUNG WOMEN THEME

In the summer of 1791 in Paris, France, King Louis XVI and Queen Marie Antoinette saw their fifteen-year reign coming to a sudden and unstoppable end, bringing the centuries-old era of absolute monarchies to an apparent and abrupt close. King Louis was misguided in thinking that he was well supported by his subjects, who had actually grown tired of the indecisive king and mounted momentum for a revolution. Louis and Antoinette had one living son at the time who was just an eight–year-old boy. Their son, Louis Charles, was next in line to be king, though sadly for the young prince, his coronation would never come.

The cost of revolution was steep for the royal family that summer. In June, the royal family attempted to go into hiding but were quickly caught and placed on house arrest. The events of July and August led to the complete overthrowing of the monarchy and ended in September when Louis XVI met the guillotine. Just four months later, young Louis Charles would be left an orphan after his mother Marie Antoinette met the same tragic fate as her husband.

Left an orphan at just ten years old, young Louis Charles was recognized by the handful of remaining royalists as the new king of

France. Not willing to allow any thought of a continued monarchy, revolutionaries kidnapped the young boy and cruelly imprisoned him. Under the de facto government, the Reign of Terror imposed violence and fearmongering to maintain its newfound control. Locked up under this regime, the young king became subject to a shoemaker named Antoine Simon, whose task it was to make a commoner out of the coronated. To eliminate the element of royalty, Simon sought to expose the young boy to the tawdry and vulgar, teaching him the language of soldiers, giving him alcohol, and entreating him to all manner of moral decay.

Young Louis rejected each attempt at his reeducation and instead subjected himself to the torture of his calloused caretakers whose ultimate neglect led to the death of young Louis after just two years in captivity. While his death was tragic, young Louis was victorious in his commitment to his cause. Refusing to turn his back on his royal heritage, legend has it that the young boy stood tall in the face of his great adversity. With each overture of opposition that was offered him, the young boy proclaimed that he could not participate because he was, in fact, of a royal heritage. The boy was born to be a king.

What gave this young boy, never-to-be king, the power to stand tall in the face of both great isolation and opposition? A clear and steady understanding of his noble identity gave him confidence to stand as a witness of his royal birthright.

Like the young king, we too live in a day of great isolation and adversity. It is equally essential for both young men and young women to stand as witnesses of our own divine royal heritage. Priesthood power is God's power, and it is intended to be leveraged by both women and men to allow them to stand as witnesses of Christ to together bless all of God's children.

In his 1988 book *The Power Within Us*, President Russell M. Nelson clearly outlined the source, purpose, and potential of God's power: "The source of our spiritual power is the Lord. The ultimate source of spiritual power is God our Father. The messenger of this power is the Holy Ghost. This power differs from electrical power. An electrical appliance consumes power, while the use of God's spiritual power replenishes our power. While electrical power can be used only for measured periods of time, spiritual power can be used for time and eternity."[1]

Spiritual power is the manifestation of priesthood power. This truth is evident as we compare the Young Men and Young Women themes that were introduced in 2019. Side by side the two themes sustain one another in their uniquely appointed roles, standing tall in their collective commitment to serve the Savior. Spiritual power is readily available to both young men and young women as they live their respective themes and strive to be disciples of Jesus Christ.

While most of our study has focused on the role of young men within the Aaronic Priesthood, young women also have an important place in harnessing Aaronic Priesthood power. As the father of three daughters, I am reminded regularly of the priesthood thread that ties fathers and daughters together. As I have watched my own daughters dedicate their lives to living the elements of the Young Women theme, I have observed real spiritual power in action. Their dedication to discipleship demonstrates the potential of their own spiritual power to bless not only other young women but also young men, parents, and families as they promote priesthood power and prepare God's children for the blessings of priesthood ordinances. With the perspective that priesthood covenants are available in their fulness only when worthy men and women are joined together at an altar in the temple, the role of the preparatory priesthood to prepare, motivate, and inspire both young men and young women for temple covenants comes into much greater focus.

While young women do not hold the Aaronic Priesthood, they do hold tremendous potential to both prepare themselves and to inspire the active priesthood participation of their young men counterparts for temple blessings. Furthermore, like deacons, teachers, and priests, by embracing the preparatory programs organized by church leaders, young women can also activate the power of covenants protecting and preparing their families for the promises of the Lord.

With the introduction of the new Young Women theme, I was among the many who were grateful to see preserved six words that defined the character of the prior generation of young women: "Stand as a witness of God."

Consider for a moment what it means to you to "stand as a witness of God." I have identified a few ideas of what it means to me.

- A witness of God is someone who lives their life in a way that provides evidence and testimony of our Heavenly Father and His Son Jesus Christ.
- A witness of God is someone through whom we feel of God's love and know of His power.
- A witness of God is someone whose actions and demeanor inspire us to want to be more than we are.
- Ultimately, a witness of God inspires us to seek out our Savior, to prepare to make and keep our own sacred covenants that enable us to draw closer to God because of how we feel when we are close to those who stand tall as His witnesses.

Think with me for a moment of the significance of having such witnesses among us in the world today. What a tremendous strength to our homes, families, and society at large to have true witnesses of God, people who have come to know the Lord for themselves and whose demeanor and actions testify of the power of the divine. Standing for truth and righteousness, these witnesses are committed to holding up their light by example—shining forth that they may set the Lord's standard for the nations to look upon for peace, happiness, and strength.

Joseph Smith offered to David Whitmer perhaps the best admonition to stand as a witness when he offered this promise: "And it shall come to pass, that if you shall ask the Father in my name, in faith believing, you shall receive the Holy Ghost, which giveth utterance, that you may *stand as a witness* of the things of which you shall both hear and see, and also that you may declare repentance unto this generation. Behold, I am Jesus Christ, the Son of the living God, who created the heavens and the earth, a light which cannot be hid in darkness" (D&C 14:8–9; emphasis added).

In this verse the Lord cites the role of those who "stand as a witness." I think it is interesting to see the reference to the Aaronic

Priesthood key of repentance. In effect, one cannot stand as a witness of Jesus Christ without testifying of the saving principles and ordinances upheld by Aaronic Priesthood keys. In short, the Lord's Aaronic Priesthood purpose to deliver repentance is fulfilled as all of His children, both women and men, stand as witnesses of Jesus Christ.

The theme that a new generation of our young women will now broadly embrace sounds a triumphant cry to the world proclaiming their witness of Jesus Christ:

> I am a beloved daughter of Heavenly Parents,
> with a divine nature and eternal destiny.
>
> As a disciple of Jesus Christ, I strive to become like Him. I seek and act upon personal revelation and minister to others in His holy name.
>
> I will stand as a witness of God at all times and
> in all things and in all places.
>
> As I strive to qualify for exaltation, I cherish the gift of repentance and seek to improve each day. With faith, I will strengthen my home and family, make and keep sacred covenants, and receive the ordinances and blessings of the holy temple.[2]

What a blessing to have a framework that helps our young women to build a relationship with their Heavenly Father sufficient to allow them to stand as witnesses of God to sustain the Aaronic Priesthood keys of repentance, baptism, and the ministry of angels and to prepare them to make sacred priesthood covenants in the temple. To me, both the Young Women and Young Men themes have been designed to support and accentuate the preparatory purposes of the Aaronic Priesthood. In so doing, the key purpose of their preparation is to qualify a young man for the Melchizedek Priesthood so that he can one day find a righteous and similarly prepared young woman and be sealed to her in the temple.

Remember that priesthood power is the power to become like our Heavenly Father. As a young woman in the Church learns to stand as a witness of God, she develops the attributes and qualities requisite for her to come to know the Savior, thus enabling her to develop an intimate familiarity with His power—even to the extent that she can stand tall as a witness of him at *all* times and in *all* things and in *all* places.

As His divinely appointed witnesses, God has deliberately blessed girls and women with the tremendous power of influence. Within their capacity to influence others for good, young women who are mindful of the power and purpose of Aaronic Priesthood ordinances can influence and invite God's children to participate in the power offered through the preparatory priesthood.

I know of a woman who joined the Church in her late teens. Before she was baptized, she accepted invitations to participate with her friends in Young Women activities. Through the influence of her peers, who stood as witnesses of God at all times, she was drawn to the preparatory gospel of repentance and baptism. As faithful daughters of their Father in Heaven, these girls recognized the need to exercise their faith on their friend's behalf. In the same week that this sincere young woman quietly contemplated the decision to be baptized and prayed for a witness from heaven, her covenanted friends, who were not aware that she was so diligently seeking an answer from heaven, fasted together that she would find the desire and courage to be baptized. Through their collective faith, these young women had exercised their divinely appointed influence in a way that brought the blessings of Aaronic Priesthood power to someone they loved.

While a woman's influence is a powerful attribute of priesthood power that can be used to bring about the ordinances of the gospel, our society today seems to embrace the seemingly far more common and contrasting currency of seduction and immorality. Consider the following quote from Elder M. Russell Ballard:

> It is unfortunately, all too easy to illustrate the confusion and distortion of womanhood in contemporary society. Immodest, immoral, intemperate women jam the airwaves, monopolize magazines, and slink across movie screens—all while being celebrated by the world. The Apostle Paul spoke prophetically of "perilous times" that will come in the last days and specifically referenced something that may have

> seemed particularly perilous to him: "silly women laden with sins, led away with divers lusts" (2 Timothy 3:1, 6). Popular culture today often makes women look silly, inconsequential, mindless and powerless. It objectifies them and disrespects them and then suggests that they are able to leave their mark on mankind only by seduction—easily the most pervasively dangerous message the adversary sends to women about themselves.[3]

With these contrasting outcomes of such a powerful attribute, what are we to do? The world is a better place when filled with witnesses of God confident and comfortable in their capacity to administer their influence. The silly young woman objectified and disrespected is replaced by a young woman who demands dignity while preserving the mysteries that God has entrusted only to her. I invite you to think with me for a moment of how both Aaronic and Melchizedek priesthood power can be sustained by righteous young women in our families, schools, and neighborhoods.

Just like Aaronic Priesthood holders whose priesthood power is often drawn from simple actions, the sustaining, righteous influence of a young woman is also often accomplished in the simplest acts that witness of God and His matchless love and power. I have been personally blessed by the nobility of these simple sustaining witnesses of God within my own family. As you pause to pay attention to the righteous women in your life, I am confident that you will also see how their witness of God has similarly invited and sustained God's power in your own life.

While on a plane with my family heading for a vacation, I sat with my head buried in my computer when my wife nudged me to look across the aisle. I looked over and saw my fourteen-year-old daughter sitting with headphones on—checked out from the world around her. What was different, however, was that open on her tray table was her heavy set of scriptures. In that moment, quietly and without fanfare, she witnessed to me of her testimony of God's love and of her commitment to come to know Him. Without saying a word or seeking attention, in that moment priesthood power was strengthened in our family as both her mother and father felt the power of God distill upon our daughter. In that moment, we were both inspired and uplifted by the powerful strength of her witness. We felt a deep sense of gratitude. As her dad, I felt a deep desire to be worthy to help provide her with the priesthood power and blessings that she was so earnestly seeking. Her quiet effort may have only been as simple as keeping her commitment to complete a personal goal, or perhaps it was something much more focused. Either way, I was uplifted and motivated to be a more worthy father and priesthood holder for her. I was inspired to partake of the gift of repentance and come unto Christ. In that moment, I also silently prayed that somewhere a righteous Aaronic Priesthood holder with a similar focus and desire to stand as a witness of God was in that moment preparing equally for the day when they might enter the temple together to unite in their own priesthood covenants with the Lord.

President Gordon B. Hinckley once stated with his customary wink and a smile, "The girl you marry will take a terrible chance on you. She will give her all to the young man she marries. He will largely determine the remainder of her life."

He continued: "The girl you marry can expect you to come to the marriage altar absolutely clean. She can expect you to be a young man of virtue in thought and word and deed. . . .

"You cannot give to your companion a greater gift than that of a marriage in God's holy house, under the protective wing of the sealing covenant of eternal marriage."[4]

As Aaronic Priesthood holders, you must be cognizant at all times that somewhere, there is a girl who is in preparation to one day take that "terrible chance" on you. What a beautiful blessing to contemplate the preparation of two souls to come together equally yoked in their commitment to the gospel of Jesus Christ. It is a miracle that can only be wrought by the Master. With diligent preparation and proven discipleship, you can have faith that a young woman is being prepared to be your perfect complement. While in your younger years, you can begin to identify the Christlike attributes found in a dedicated disciple amongst the young women with whom you associate. You will find them capable of inspiring you to be your very best self.

Young women hold a unique position to directly influence the power of Aaronic Priesthood holders in their neighborhoods, wards, and schools. As young women come to understand the magnitude that a true witness of God can have on Aaronic Priesthood holders, they will learn to leverage their example and testimony to accomplish the purposes of the Lord. Again, let me indulge with a personal illustration of one young woman's righteous influence on me as she quietly fulfilled her commitment to shun the temptations of the world and stand as a witness of God.

As a young man at age seventeen, I found myself often mixed up with friends who were caught up in the confusion of contemporary society, at times catching ourselves conversing in ways that were not becoming of the Aaronic Priesthood holders we had been ordained to be. During this time, I made friends with a girl of my same age who I soon began to like. She was far from immodest or immoral. In her family she had been taught and internalized the gospel of Jesus Christ. She was keenly aware that her influence in the world was founded on a divine heritage supported by truth and righteousness that was as limitless as her Heavenly Father is eternal.

As I became better friends with this young woman, I found myself embarrassed by the conversations I found myself participating in while in her presence. I felt within myself a desire to be attractive to her. I knew that to become so, I would need to change. I needed to repent. Without saying a word, her righteous demeanor along with her quiet demand for dignity had a tremendous influence on me.

Ultimately, it was in part through my friendship with this young woman and her positive influence that I decided to make the proper adjustments in my own life that would lead me to better prepare myself for the Melchizedek Priesthood and to make sacred covenants with my Heavenly Father. Several years later, I found myself immensely grateful and happy to be in the temple with that same young woman making sacred covenants to stand for truth and righteousness together with her for eternity. Today, she continues to stand as a witness of God that invites and sustains the priesthood power that we need to bless our family.

Whether as Aaronic Priesthood holders, mothers, fathers, siblings, extended family members, friends, leaders, or others, we all hold a sacred obligation to support and protect our young women and to encourage their role as witnesses of God. Young women have a sacred obligation to make their world a more beautiful and holier place through the power of their influence. The potential for young women to influence the world for good is without limit. A young woman's influence is divinely appointed to both sustain and prepare the way for priesthood power to bless God's children as she stands as a witness of God at all times, in all things, and in all places and prepares herself to make covenants in the temple.

When Aaronic Priesthood holders and young women recognize that the Lord's purposes are best accomplished when they unify priesthood keys with divinely appointed influence, together they cultivate true spiritual power. By retaining a deep sense of their individual divine identity, they can stand together as witnesses of God, fulfilling their uniquely respective roles to do the work of the covenants and administer the ordinances of salvation. As dedicated disciples of Jesus Christ, they will be ready to fulfill the purposes of his preparatory priesthood—one day dressed in white and kneeling at an altar, as children of heavenly parents, a people prepared for the coming of the Lord.

NOTES

1. Russell M. Nelson, *The Power Within Us* (Salt Lake City: Deseret Book, 1988).
2. Young Women Theme, The Church of Jesus Christ of Latter-day Saints, 2019.
3. M. Russell Ballard, "Mothers and Daughters," *Ensign*, May 2010.
4. Gordon B. Hinckley, "Living Worthy of the Girl You Will Someday Marry," churchofjesuschrist.org/study/general-conference/1998/04/living-worthy-of-the-girl-you-will-someday-marry?lang=eng. Accessed May 26, 2020.

SONS AND DAUGHTERS OF HEAVENLY PARENTS

Preparing a People for the Coming of the Lord

DOCTRINE

Read the Young Women and Young Men themes.
Look for elements that support both young men's and young women's divinely appointed purposes in sustaining what you have learned about the Aaronic Priesthood keys of repentance, baptism, and the ministry of angels.

Read "Living Worthy of the Girl You Will Someday Marry" by President Gordon B. Hinckley (General Conference, Priesthood Session, April 1998.)
Look for attributes of a worthy husband and father that you feel are important for you to develop now.

PRINCIPLE

Together with members of your family or quorum, discuss what it means to stand as a witness of God.

Together with members of your family or quorum, compare and contrast both themes.

Discuss what they have in common and what is different. Evaluate together the unique purposes that have been laid out in the themes for young men and young women.

Together with members of your family or quorum, discuss what you can do now to prepare yourself for the girl you will someday marry.

Together with members of your quorum, plan an activity or other initiative that you can do together to include the young women you know in fulfilling the purposes of the Aaronic Priesthood.

THEORY

Write about the following in your journal:

- Commitments you will make now to sustain young women with whom you associate in their commitment to stand as witnesses of God.
- Specific attributes that you want to develop to ensure that you are well prepared to be a worthy husband and father.
- Specific attributes that both you and Heavenly Father value in a worthy wife and mother.

PART II

To My Great Joy

Helaman's Patterns for Powerful Priesthood Leaders

But behold, to my great joy, there had not one soul of them fallen.

—ALMA 56:56

In the Book of Mormon, the prophet Helaman proved to be an incredible mentor, adviser, and leader for the stripling men over whom he had stewardship. While Helaman's two thousand sons are oft noted for what their mothers had taught them, it was Helaman who courageously facilitated their success in battle with his preparations and strategies.

The account of Helaman and his brave warriors is detailed in an epistle sent by Helaman to the Nephi captain Moroni chronicled in Alma 56. Helaman was the great Aaronic Priesthood leader and is a wonderful resource for all Aaronic Priesthood holders as well as the leaders who mentor and train them in their homes, quorums, and wards. Helaman provides priesthood holders with several patterns for priesthood leadership that can be instrumental in producing powerful quorums inspired with courage and confidence to fulfill their purpose of preparing people for the coming of the Lord.

I invite you to open your Book of Mormon and carefully read chapter 56. As you read, look for the patterns of genuine love, mentoring, successful service, providing provisions, his call for courage, and other patterns that Helaman sets as he positions these young men to fulfill their potential. These patterns can be adopted by Aaronic Priesthood quorum members, presidencies, parents, leaders, and advisers to develop strong quorums and priesthood holders who are prepared for the coming of the Lord.

You will likely very quickly recall the story of the two thousand stripling warriors. Helaman was a captain in the Nephite army charged by Captain Moroni to protect the Anti-Nephi-Lehies, a Lamanite people who had been converted by the great missionary Ammon and who had covenanted to never again take up arms against another. They left behind their Lamanite traditions to move to the land of Zarahemla, where they could live in peace under the protection of the Nephites.

However, as Lamanite forces grew, threatening the Nephites, the Anti-Nephi-Lehies became concerned and considered breaking their covenant to join the Nephite army in order to prepare for battle against the Lamanites. Recognizing the plight of their parents and their need for protection, and at the urging of the Nephite captain, Helaman, these sons of the Anti-Nephi-Lehies felt the solemn responsibility to support their parents in their commitment to keep their covenants. They volunteered themselves to join Helaman in forming an army that could protect and preserve the Nephites. Under Helaman's patterns for leadership, this band of brothers grew in strength and confidence, taking upon them the name of Nephites. They were prepared to preserve their people in their covenants for the coming of the Lord.

"They were all young men, and they were exceedingly valiant for courage, and also for strength and activity; but behold, this was not all—they were men who were true at all times in whatsoever thing they were entrusted. Yea, they were men of truth and soberness, for they had been taught to keep the commandments of God and to walk uprightly before him" (Alma 53:20–21).

In the opening paragraphs of his epistle to Moroni, Helaman proudly states that he has "somewhat to tell you concerning our warfare in this part of the land." He recognizes that what he has experienced is nothing small and that it is even miraculous. I love that he uses the word "somewhat." I like to think of him telling Moroni, "Get comfortable, I am about to tell you an unbelievable tale." As Moroni settles in to read this great epistle, Helaman articulates the first of his patterns for powerful quorums by identifying his own priesthood purpose.

A Pattern of Love

For they are worthy to be called sons.

Helaman loved these young men dearly. He understood who they were and reminded them regularly of their place as heirs of covenant-making parents. He begins by reacquainting Moroni with his band of soldiers by reminding him of their origin. The stripling warriors were the sons of the Anti-Nephi-Lehies whom Ammon had brought from the land of Nephi. He points out that they were descendants of Laman. He is not shy about explaining to Moroni that he does not need to retell the tradition of unbelief that had generally prevailed among the Lamanites.

While acknowledging the Lamanites' history of wickedness, Helaman is also quick to remember that these young men are the sons of the repentant Anti-Nephi-Lehies who have made a covenant to never again take up their weapons to shed the blood of another man. Helaman is clear in his understanding that these covenant people were at their breaking point. Without a military intervention, they would be forced to choose between breaking their covenants and certain death and destruction. In this clarity of thought, Helaman finds purpose when he says: "*But I would not suffer them that they should break this covenant which they had made*, supposing that God would strengthen us, insomuch that we should not suffer more because of the fulfilling the oath which they had taken" (Alma 56:8; emphasis added).

In short, Helaman articulates his priesthood purpose to protect the covenants of the people. He boldly states that nobody is going to break a covenant with the Lord on his watch. Furthermore, Helaman demonstrates great faith that the Lord will not only strengthen this people, but also that this repentant people would not have to suffer further persecution on account of their covenant with God. Helaman's love for his soldiers and understanding of his role and purpose as their leader is summed up later in his epistle when he acknowledges the hand of the Lord with this simple but beautiful expression of gratitude: "And thus were we favored of the Lord" (Helaman 56:19).

Like Helaman, it is imperative that you are able to establish a clear purpose in your service as an Aaronic Priesthood holder and, when called upon, as a leader in your quorum. You can do this by following Helaman's example to know well and to love the quorum members you serve. As you develop an individual love for the members of your quorum, it becomes easy to see clearly your unique purpose to contribute to the strengthening of your quorum.

Helaman took time to learn not only who his young men were but from where they came. He knew that they were descendants of a people who had a long tradition of wickedness and that within their lineage there had been a generational repentance and a dramatic shift to righteousness. He knew that they had been raised at the feet of parents who possessed a powerful testimony of Christ's Atonement, having heard their stories of repentance that accompanied the burial of their swords. Certainly, he felt the power of that transformation and saw the potential that they each had as young men of testimony, integrity, faith, and virtue. Helaman understood clearly the generational influence of the preparatory gospel. He recognized the precious opportunity these young men had been given to help prepare their covenanted parents for the coming of the Lord by their commitment to take up arms so that their fathers did not have to. In providing this parental protection and preparation, Helaman saw clearly that these young men would prepare themselves to follow the example of their parents by entering into their own priesthood covenants. Through his commitment to them, he developed a sincere and certainly individual love for each of his sons.

Like these soldiers, young men need to know that their Aaronic Priesthood leaders and advisers are, like Helaman, committed to always being there, to being invested in their priesthood progress, to loving them. Essential trust can only be garnered as young men are provided sufficient predictability to allow them to have a firm foundation upon which they can discover a unique purpose for their own priesthood ministry and service. This predictability is most effective when established through quorum presidencies and supported by advisers.

Consider with me a few different ways that predictability can help the members of your quorum to identify their own priesthood purpose and draw closer to the Savior.

A quorum presidency that is committed to a regular meeting schedule will find the time to plan and prepare for the needs of quorum members. Love will grow when your quorum presidency is able to establish predictable patterns for counseling together and establishing personalized priesthood priorities.

A quorum that has frequent campouts and other high adventure activities provides consistent opportunities for young men to share unique experiences. These types of activities will challenge their physical and emotional strength. When these activities occur only sporadically, it can be more difficult for quorum members to have the necessary confidence in themselves and their quorum relationships. Without regularity, it can be difficult for some quorum members to commit to participating, which can rob them of opportunities to grow. Brotherly love is nurtured when quorums regularly share unique outdoor experiences.

Love will grow when a quorum submits to shared spiritual experiences. When a quorum places as priority spiritually nurturing activities such as gospel study, ministering, and temple service, they qualify themselves to receive the Holy Ghost. As your quorum presidency recognizes that conversion is conditioned on consistency, you will discover meaningful ways to create opportunities to come to know the Savior together.

President Gordon B. Hinckley used to speak of the constant nature of the Polar Star and likened it to love, referring to love as the "lodestar of life." He spoke of nights sleeping out with his brother when they "came to know the constancy of that star. As the earth turned, the others appeared to move through the night. But the North Star held its position in line with the axis of the earth. And so, it had come to be known as the Polar Star, or the Polestar, or the Lodestar.

Hinckley said, "Through centuries of time, mariners had used it to guide them in their journeys. They had reckoned their bearings by its constancy, thereby avoiding traveling in circles or in the wrong direction, as they moved across the wide, unmarked seas."

President Hinckley continued:

> Because of those boyhood musings, the Polar Star came to mean something to me. I recognized it as a constant in the midst of change. It was something that could always be counted on, something that was dependable, an anchor in what otherwise appeared to be a moving and unstable firmament.
>
> Love is like the Polar Star. In a changing world, it is a constant. It is of the very essence for the gospel. It is the security of the home. It is the safeguard of community life. It is a beacon of hope in a world of distress.[1]

Just like the young President Hinckley, young men of today quietly yearn for the dependable anchor that genuine love provides. Whether you are a fellow quorum member, quorum presidency member, adviser, bishop, or perhaps a parent, each of us as covenant members of Christ's church are charged with sustaining the preparatory priesthood in its purpose to preserve and protect the saving ordinances of the preparatory gospel. With love as our lodestar, our purpose becomes clear.

As we invest in coming to understand who the individual holders of the Aaronic Priesthood are and even from whom they have descended, we will begin to see them as Helaman saw his army. We will know them not only by name but also from where they have come and to where they are going. We will begin to see who they can become and what they can accomplish in the Lord. Anchored by life's lodestar, we will find purpose in our service.

Like both Helaman and the mariners of old, we will have the necessary vision to help them clearly chart their course and guide them in their service. Most of all, we will develop the same love for them that warranted Helaman to refer to his soldiers as sons, which in turn allowed for them to love him as a father. Out of this understanding, like their heroic captain, leaders will feel a deep desire and a defined sense of purpose to sustain quorum members in the duty that is uniquely theirs—to become as the armies of Helaman—protecting their families in their covenants and preparing through their ministry for all of God's children to receive their Savior.

NOTE

1. Gordon B. Hinckley, "Let Love Be the Lodestar of Your Life," churchofjesuschrist.org/study/general-conference/1989/04/let-love-be-the-lodestar-of-your-life?lang=eng. Accessed May 26, 2020.

A Pattern of Successful Service

And thus we were prepared.

With a clear understanding of the true identity and the priesthood potential of his young army, and with love as his lodestar, Helaman was blessed with both the vision to clearly see the necessary course to maximize their capabilities and the confidence to place them on a path that would only result in successful service.

Helaman knew that his soldiers were young. He knew not only of their potential, but certainly he was familiar with the limitations of their youth. In verses 9 through 16, as Helaman charged himself to lead this band of brethren, it is noteworthy to pay attention to the first mission that Helaman organized for his young army.

Wisely, Helaman did not lead them immediately into a fierce battle with the strongest of the Lamanite armies. Instead, he recognized that one of the Nephite captains, Antipus, was weary and forlorn because of the losses that he had conceded to the Lamanites. Sufficiently in-tune to recognize the opportunity for successful service, Helaman organized his young army and gave them a manageable mission that did not exceed the measure of their preparation and capacity.

In his epistle to Moroni, after acknowledging the many losses that had been suffered across a multitude of the Nephite cities, Helaman writes that despite fighting valiantly, Antipus and his soldiers were "depressed in body as well as in spirit," having "suffered great afflictions of every kind" (Alma 56:16).

Thus, having knowledge of their vulnerable state, Helaman seized an opportunity to not only provide relief but also to challenge his "little force" within the confines of their confidence and capacity. Rather than sending them immediately to face their enemies, Helaman simply sent his sons to their allies in Antipus and his army, where they could experience success in their service by giving "great hopes and much joy" (Alma 56:17) to the weary soldiers.

This simple act increased the confidence of Antipus and his army by giving his soldiers hope and even "much joy." Better yet was that as the Lamanites saw the new spring in the step of Antipus, they were subsequently "compelled by the orders of Ammoron to not come against [them] to battle (Alma 56:18)."

Take a small step back with me and observe what happened here. Helaman, knowing that his army was young and inexperienced, gave them a task that was easy for them—he basically asked them to simply show up. Just by their presence, they buoyed up the beleaguered army of Antipus and in so doing established an important relationship with the more seasoned soldiers.

Think for a moment of the joy that the young soldiers must have felt as they were received by the more experienced, albeit exhausted, army of Antipus. Consider how these little brothers were suddenly validated in their service. Furthermore, imagine how this confidence would have been immensely magnified upon learning of Ammoron's orders to not come against them.

This "little force" immediately experienced an immense increase in their confidence. Certainly, courage began to replace caution as this band of boys grew in their preparation. I like to think of the men in Antipus's army not only receiving them with joy but also taking time to mentor the young soldiers and to share their own personal experiences from the battlefield. I think that these experienced soldiers were likely quick to give all the credit to their younger counterparts for Ammoron's decision to hold back the Lamanite forces. I like to think of Helaman's warriors being told by these battle-tested men that they too could do it, that they could serve just as valiantly, that they too could find the courage and faith to be the heroes that their families so desperately needed. Strengthened by their "victory" and with the confidence instilled by the army of Antipus, Helaman's little force had been well prepared to accept even greater priesthood assignments.

Had Helaman failed to observe the opportunity to facilitate successful priesthood service, had he simply yelled "charge!" and sent them forth with swords gleaming, I think that it would be very unlikely for us to know much of anything about these valiant young men. Instead, Helaman recognized both the potential and the inexperience that these young soldiers possessed. To his credit, he charted a course that ensured an outcome in which they grew in knowledge, testimony, confidence, and character.

How often are Aaronic Priesthood leaders presented with similar opportunities to facilitate successful priesthood service? We have likely all participated in priesthood service that has not gone well. Perhaps we have been part of an underwhelming force of teachers who stayed after church to put chairs away. Or, possibly as a quorum president you are all too familiar with the sinking feeling that comes at the beginning of an Aaronic Priesthood presidency meeting when you look around and only see your adviser present with no sign of your counselors and secretary.

As Aaronic Priesthood leaders it can be easy to blame unsuccessful priesthood experiences on our fellow Aaronic Priesthood holders' inexperience, disinterest, and distraction, along with a host of other excuses. It is easy catch ourselves saying things such as "Priests are just too busy with work, school, sports, and girls to be engaged in Aaronic Priesthood activities." Or, "Getting teachers out of bed for an early morning service project is impossible." Similarly, it can be easy to become frustrated with quorum presidencies who come to presidency meetings unprepared and without an agenda, knowing that you will end up guiding the meeting despite your repeated efforts to tell them to come prepared.

Serving Aaronic Priesthood holders can be difficult both as a presidency member and as an adviser. But just like Helaman, success can be found when we recognize both strengths and limitations while identifying opportunities for priesthood success.

One of the key roles of an adviser is to be a coach. As a coach, you have to know the game, the boundaries, and what league you play in. Most important, a coach needs to know the players on the field.

It would be ridiculous for a high school baseball coach to show up at a tee-ball game played by five-year-olds, ready to coach and with an expectation of finding the team appropriately organized—taking fly-balls in the outfield while the infield works on double plays and the pitchers warm up in the bull-pen, all while another player takes batting practice at home plate.

Each Aaronic Priesthood quorum is organized by the age of its members, where they are grouped with others of similar maturity and priesthood potential.

Deacons come into priesthood service full of energy and enthusiasm. They are still boys ready and waiting for a mentor or coach to guide nearly every step in their service. Deacons are eager to receive assignments and very willing to serve. They need a coach who can teach priesthood fundamentals.

Teachers arrive more prepared, having learned many of the fundamentals, but are still working on becoming proficient in their service. They also are often ready to receive direction to serve but are at a place in their maturity where they are often anxious to exercise their agency.

While still maturing into manhood, priests have a significantly increased measure of accountability and capability to both organize and execute priesthood tasks and service. With limited direction they are capable of independently counseling together and allocating their collective priesthood resources to be successful in their service.

Think again of how the right coach at the tee-ball game manages his responsibilities to teach young players. At this level, the coach is teaching the most basic fundamentals of the game. He is teaching how to properly throw the ball, catch, and swing the bat. He is also teaching the basics of being part of a team, including sportsmanship and having a positive attitude. Think about where on the field you see the coach of a team at this level stand. You rarely see him seated on the sideline or in the dugout. Rather, you often see the coach right out on the field, standing in the middle of play. You may see a tee-ball coach standing right near the batter, ready to grab him by the shoulders after he hits the ball to physically point him toward first base, where you might see an assistant coach standing, waving their arms and calling for the hitter to run to the base. Maybe you have been at a game where the batter does not receive or obey this direction and instead of running to first, he makes a beeline straight to second base. Or perhaps you have seen a similar-aged soccer player score a goal in the wrong net and raise his arms in celebration.

It can be easy to assume that these young players will know exactly how to play because of their experience growing up surrounded by the game, seeing their older siblings playing, or perhaps having attended college or professional games with their families. However, in watching players at this level, we quickly realize that there is still much to learn that only comes by actually being on the field and in the game. We can easily observe that proficiency and success only come by patient and dedicated practice, seasoned by what is learned through adversity and failure.

Contrast the tee-ball coach with a high school coach. The high school coach arrives at the game ready to give direction, guidance, and encouragement. He is familiar with the individual strengths of each team member and understands clearly how to maximize each player's ability. The high school coach knows that he is no longer welcome on the field and if he crosses the boundary line, he concedes his position and is only eligible to interfere with the game. In a high school game, the players play and the coaches coach.

These coaching principles apply well to both Aaronic Priesthood leaders and advisers seeking to follow the example set by Helaman in facilitating successful priesthood service. By observing through this coaching lens, I have seen many simple examples of Aaronic Priesthood advisers, leaders, and quorum presidency members working together to harness the power of the Aaronic Priesthood to deliver successful service. I will share an example with you.

While preparing a Sunday "Come Follow Me" lesson titled "What are my duties as an Aaronic Priesthood holder?", one adviser read a scripture regarding the duties of a deacons quorum president: "The duty of a president over the office of a deacon is to preside over twelve deacons, to sit in council with them, and to teach them their duty, edifying one another, as it is given according to the covenants" (D&C 107:85).

This verse prompted the identification of an opportunity to have the deacons quorum president participate in the lesson with a deliberate effort to acknowledge his duty to teach the other quorum members their respective duties. It would have been easy to just ask the young quorum president to come prepared to teach one of the duties of the Aaronic Priesthood. However, the adviser recognized the inexperience of the quorum president and the need to "get on the field" to facilitate a successful priesthood leadership experience.

A successful leadership experience was accomplished after the adviser invited the quorum president to go to his home to discuss the lesson. They opened their discussion by reading the verse about the duties of the president "to sit in council and to teach them their duty." In the quiet moment while they read the scripture together, the young quorum president was able to be touched by the Spirit and feel the Lord speaking directly to him in articulating his important responsibility right before his eyes.

Empowered by the Holy Ghost, the quorum president was ready to discover what he could teach the quorum. With the support of his adviser, he identified a question that would guide not only the lesson preparation but also the planning of many activities and lessons from that day forward: "As we plan this lesson/activity, in what ways will the Aaronic Priesthood holders learn that their work is essential to the work of God?"

Together the quorum president and the adviser organized a lesson that allowed for the quorum president to fulfill his duty of teaching the quorum and helping them to understand by the Spirit the essential nature of their service. Specifically, in this instance, the adviser helped the president develop a loose script for the lesson in which the president was able to lead a discussion with the deacons regarding the passing of the sacrament. Together he led them in reading the scripture stating that the duties of the deacon are "to expound, exhort, and teach, and invite all to come unto Christ" (D&C 20:59). With the support of the adviser, the quorum president sat at the head of a table that had been brought into the classroom that day to help create a sense of equality amongst the deacons with the advisers sitting on the outside of the circle.

Both well prepared and well rehearsed, the quorum president led a discussion about how passing the sacrament helped the deacons to fulfill their duty to warn, exhort, expound, and invite in the following ways:

- **Warn**—By demonstrating sincere reverence in dress and in the manner that the sacrament is administered, Aaronic Priesthood holders can warn ward members of the sacred nature of the sacrament and remind them of the consequences of partaking unworthily of the sacred emblems.
- **Expound**—In simple reverence, as the sacrament is distributed, doctrines of the Atonement are being expounded to those who are thoughtfully contemplating the life and sacrifice of the Savior. Without the service of the Aaronic Priesthood, this spiritual understanding is greatly stunted.
- **Exhort**—A reverently extended tray exhorts, or strongly encourages, the members to renew their covenant.
- **Invite**—Perhaps this is obvious, but by virtue of extending the opportunity to partake of the sacrament every week, the Aaronic Priesthood (including the bishop) extends an initiation for all of our Heavenly Father's children to repent and to come unto Christ.

While it would have been much easier for the adviser to simply teach these points to the deacons, the discussion was immensely more impactful when nine deacons sat around a table with their scriptures open, led by one who was exercising keys that only he possessed. Led by the quorum president, they collectively connected the dots between their weekly service assignment and the doctrines outlined by the Lord. This resulted in a far richer discussion.

Through it all, the adviser had been "on the field" coaching and demonstrating how to lead the discussion before stepping off and leaving the ball with his trusted team captain who was both prepared and capable to lead the young team to victory. This style of coaching enabled the deacons to gain a much deeper understanding for themselves of how their work is essential to accomplishing God's priesthood purposes.

These types of experiences can and should be prevalent within our quorums. The catalyst for accomplishing these types of results is time spent before the game—in practice. An effective adviser understands that his primary responsibility is to train quorum leaders to be effective in their service. The more an adviser understands his role, the more he will see that some of his most impactful service will occur outside of quorum meetings and sometimes even outside of presidency meetings.

Helaman understood well this concept of pregame preparation. Following the successful mission to buoy up the army of Antipus, Helaman was again perceptive in recognizing how to leverage the latest measure of preparation by his young army. After recognizing that Ammoron had ordered his army to withhold their attack, Helaman led his army to prepare the city and themselves for defense, noting that the young army was "not desirous to make an attack upon (the Lamanites) in their strongholds" (Helaman 56:21).

Again, Helaman was wise to know that his young force needed to be prepared for battle on their own ground and terms. By preparing their defenses within the safety of their own city, the young sons would again invest additional time well spent in preparation.

In recounting this subtle detail of the preparation of Helaman's army, I am reminded again of the wise bishop who saw the opportunity for his priests quorum to prepare their own defenses by visiting the homes of ward members and sharing with them their elementary-level *Preach My Gospel* lessons. The bishop, like Helaman, saw the value in preparing the Lord's army within the safety of his own city where the costs of defeat were very low. The bishop knew that giving his priests the opportunity to learn the lessons and practice teaching within the ward would not only help the young men but would also assist to build up the defenses of the families in the ward. Moreover, the bishop was perceptive to see that each nervous young man would also have the opportunity to experience some of the anxiety-inducing aspects of missionary work on the front steps of a neighbor across the street in preparation for a future day when he would stand with increased confidence on a lonely porch somewhere across the world.

Like Helaman and the bishop, all Aaronic Priesthood leaders and advisers can look for opportunities to help Aaronic Priesthood holders prepare their own defenses against the deafening whispers of the adversary and his confidence-crushing manipulation of mortality.

Knowing full well the rigors of missionary service, a thoughtful adviser will be quick to observe opportunities to strengthen aspiring Melchizedek Priesthood holders and will be committed to make time to mentor. Like Helaman, the effective adviser will assist quorum members and leaders in both learning and carrying out their duties. He will help them to understand the blessings that they can bring to others and will help them see clearly the blessings that priesthood service can bring to them personally. He will find opportunities for his young quorum to receive confidence and mentoring from older soldiers, perhaps those who have served as full-time missionaries. Furthermore, an effective adviser will follow the example of Helaman to facilitate opportunities for the Aaronic Priesthood to inspire hope and bring joy to those blessed through its service. He will work constantly to not underestimate or overcompensate for the power of this "little force" to accomplish the Lord's purposes.

As they look to make constant connections between commonplace priesthood assignments and the underlying doctrines of the priesthood, effective quorum presidency members and advisers will find themselves blessed with increased capacity to facilitate successful priesthood experiences. With a steady focus on the Lord's intended role for Aaronic Priesthood holders to exercise their keys of the ministering of angels and to deliver the gospel of repentance and baptism, an effective quorum presidency supported by a visionary adviser will find that just as the Lord showed Helaman, he will also show Aaronic Priesthood leaders a clear path and achievable tasks that will facilitate successful priesthood service. This priesthood service will allow quorum members to grow in confidence as they prepare their own defenses and deliver the sustaining power of the Savior's Atonement to those whom they serve.

A Pattern to Magnify Parents

Now ye also know of the covenant which their fathers made.

Upheld by the love of their captain and sustained by the support of those whom they had served, Helaman's army had their feet shod with the preparation of the gospel of peace and were protected by the whole armor of God. However, even with their excellent preparation, our hero Helaman knew that the battle ahead would warrant more of his men than even he could provide. He understood clearly the power of having purpose that came from deep within each soldier's heart. Helaman knew that the real power to overcome the enemy would be found in family.

Rarely is a Mother's Day talk given in a sacrament meeting that does not rightfully reference the powerful influence that mothers had on the sons of Helaman. In writing to Moroni, Helaman attributes the success of the young soldiers' ability to overcome all fear despite their inexperience because of what they had "been taught by their mothers," knowing that "if they did not doubt, God would deliver them"—even rehearsing to Helaman the words of their mothers, saying, "We do not doubt our mothers knew it" (Alma 56:47–48).

While the mothers are often the most heralded in this story, the equally important role of the fathers of these young sons is often overlooked. Earlier in Helaman's account, following the success of the first mission to support the army of Antipus, Helaman's army was tasked with building up the defenses of the city of Judea where they were stationed with the soldiers of Antipus. Not wanting to attack the Lamanites in their strongholds, Helaman's strategy was for his army to prepare themselves for what they thought was an inevitable attack by the Lamanites. In anticipation, Helaman maintained spies to watch for Lamanite activity. Their strategy was to wait for the Lamanite armies to pass by the well-equipped city of Judea on their way to more vulnerable Nephite cities, at which time the armies of Helaman and Antipus could descend from Judea to attack the Lamanites from behind.

However, just as not every quorum campout goes exactly as planned, Helaman's strategy was not effective and failed to meet his expectations. The Lamanites were wise to the strategy and recognized that in attacking the weaker cities they too would be in a vulnerable position. Despite the ill-fated stratagem, Helaman's young army could at least take credit for, albeit inadvertently, deterring the Lamanite forces from making an attack.

With neither side wanting to make the first mistake by leaving their cities to attack the other in their strongholds, the war grew into somewhat of a stalemate. Certainly, Helaman's army grew weary as they watched their supplies and provisions dwindle.

For years, I had skimmed this story and knew clearly how these stripling warriors had been inspired with testimony, faith, and courage by their mothers. However, it was not until one inspired evening while reading this chapter that the saving role of their fathers jumped off the page to catch my attention: "In the second month of this year, there was brought unto us many provisions *from the fathers* of those my two thousand sons" (Alma 56:27; emphasis added).

Consistent with God's eternal plan for the divinely appointed roles of fathers and mothers, we see clearly that the sons of Helaman had been born to parents who shared in the "solemn responsibility to love and care for each other and for their children . . . hav[ing] a sacred duty to rear their children in love and righteousness, to provide for their physical and spiritual needs, and to teach them to love and serve one another, observe the commandments of God, and be law-abiding citizens wherever they live."[1]

Heavenly Father's plan for families is eternal and was evident in Helaman's day just as it is today. Helaman's sons had mothers who were "primarily responsible for the nurture of their children"[2] and fathers whose duty it was "by divine design, to preside over their families in love and righteousness and [were] responsible to provide the necessities of life and protection for their families."[3] Both mothers and fathers understood clearly that they were "obligated to help one another as equal partners."[4]

It is inspiring to consider how the sons of Helaman were nurtured with love and testimony by their mothers while their fathers stood by as noble providers ready to buoy them up with the provisions necessary for their success, all while honoring the exercise of agency by their young sons to courageously protect the freedom of their families. While staying true to their commitment to not take up weapons of their own, humbly and faithfully these fathers and mothers were proactive in honoring their covenants to raise up, provide for, and protect a righteous inheritance.

When our homes are presided over by fathers and mothers who take seriously their priesthood covenants, our homes are blessed by men and women who serve as surrogate Saviors to their families.

The beauty of God's plan to bring His children home is that it requires an equal measure of salvation to be facilitated by His sons and daughters as they both honor priesthood covenants in fulfilling their respective roles as providers, presiders, and nurturers in their mutual commitment to build on the foundational teachings of the Lord Jesus Christ.

In facilitating mortality, the Lord, in a very sacred way, acknowledges the role of mothers as surrogates for Christ in facilitating birth into mortal life by water, blood, and spirit. Is it not interesting to think about the sacred nature of our mortal birth and the participatory role that women share with Christ in bringing about God's plan of salvation by facilitating the arrival of a child into mortal life?

Similarly, it is interesting to note the role of earthly fathers in the second birth, or the birth into eternal life, as they officiate in the baptisms of their children where those children are born again of water, the blood of Christ, and of the Holy Ghost.

God's plan is perfect and requires the equal but different participation of men and women to become like their Savior as they serve in the respective roles as mothers and fathers to bring about the salvation of our Heavenly Father's children. Helaman set forth a pattern that magnified these sacred roles for his sons. He would have certainly discussed in detail "those things which their mothers had taught them." He also pointed them to their fathers for provisions in their moment of need. Helaman helped his young soldiers remember the power of covenanted parents to provide for and sustain their children. Helaman's efforts did not replace the role of parents. He did, however, create opportunities for observation and revelation to occur.

When parents place themselves on notice to observe, they can respond like the Anti-Nephi-Lehies in ways that will result in the preparation of a powerful priesthood prepared to accomplish the grand designs of our Heavenly Father. Here are a few simple examples of parents who magnify their capacity to serve as surrogate Saviors to their children.

Consider the twelve–year-old deacon who regularly takes his turn in family prayer. Do his parents note that he repeats the same prayer every time he prays with very little variation? Do they discuss as a family specific needs or circumstances where special blessings can be sought through sincere family prayer? Do they listen and feel the joy that comes from the Holy Ghost when that boy's prayer changes one night without compulsion to include a more meaningful conversation with his Father in Heaven to specifically bless someone in need?

Consider the fourteen–year-old young woman who comes home from church crying after being excluded by some of the older girls. Does her father blow off her concerns as teenage drama that he doesn't have time for? Or does he put an arm around her and take time to recognize her individual worth? Does her mother serve as a surrogate Savior to strengthen her feeble knees and give her the confidence to walk tall as a daughter of God? Think of how that young woman can be blessed to feel the powerful influence of a loving mother as well as a patient priesthood holder father. Consider the Aaronic Priesthood holder in that family who, through this experience, sees the gentle hand of compassion extended by his father. What might he learn about the priesthood purpose of having respect for women and girls?

Finally, think about the fifteen–year-old teacher who is discovering sexuality in unhealthy ways, including through the lens of pornography. Do his parents show him only the dance steps of repentance by giving him an awkward checklist that starts and ends with a single trip to the bishop? Or, do they rejoice at the opportunity to walk the redeeming road together in this moment when the consequences of disobedience are still very manageable? Do they serve as surrogates for the Savior and help him take advantage of this pitfall in mortality so that he can reach up and feel the wounds in the hands of the Savior? Do they walk away from their bishop's office together, having learned the song of redeeming love confidently having the image of God engraven upon their collective countenances? The mother of that troubled teacher may welcome the boy home with a plan of action that fosters a culture of transparency in her home where a newfound understanding of healthy sexuality can be pursued complete with disclosure, understanding, and accountability. She may teach the difference between the gift of God's true love and the counterfeit that is Satan's gift of lust. With God-given courage and compassion, she can plainly illustrate the difference between the isolated, compulsive, and destructive nature of lust and the inclusive, liberating, transparent, and confident nature of love. It is this love that will ultimately draw that young man to a young woman who is similarly seeking the love, joy, and peace that is obtained when "they that are Christ's [who] have crucified the flesh with the affections and lusts," come together to establish a union founded on the teachings of the Lord Jesus Christ and sealed by the tender melodies sung by the Holy Ghost (Galatians 5:19–24).

The music of the gospel is the song of redeeming love. It is the instrument that will enable our children to remember and return. Knowing his sons had been taught the music, Helaman facilitated opportunities for family relationships to flourish by sustaining sacred family responsibilities.

Just as Helaman recognized that fathers and mothers had the first responsibility for the spiritual welfare of their children, bishoprics and Aaronic Priesthood advisers share in the sacred assignment of sustaining parents and families in their covenanted responsibility to apply gospel principles at home. Aaronic Priesthood leaders are called to strengthen individuals and families. Quorum presidencies and advisers support young men in their personal effort to become converted to the gospel of Jesus Christ. They support parents in their roles when they help young men to learn and live the gospel in every aspect of their lives.

When we know our divinely appointed roles as parents and see ourselves as the surrogate Saviors that we are, we will honor the covenants that we have made to simply try to be like Him. When we remain committed in our efforts to become like Him, the sealing power will be manifest. All who stray will hear the voice of the Good Shepherd, which will be familiar to them because they will remember the sweet melodies of the gospel that were sung by their surrogate shepherds in their homes. These soft but powerful notes—this gift of the Holy Ghost—will inspire all children who wander to return home.

Like the army of Helaman, the happiness enjoyed within our families depends on parents who can deliver the necessary provisions to enable our children's ability to hear and love the beautiful music of the gospel. Being able to both hear the music along with knowing the dance steps will ultimately enable all of us to return home to live as families under a covenant of eternal happiness with our Father in Heaven.

NOTES

1. "The Family: A Proclamation to the World," *Ensign*, Nov. 2010, 129.
2. Ibid.
3. Ibid.
4. Ibid.

A Pattern of Providing Provisions to Partake of the Atonement

There was brought unto us many provisions.

One of the impressive insights gained from the story of Helaman is found in observing his commitment to ensure that his soldiers were amply supplied with the necessary provisions for their success. While calling upon their fathers, Helaman had "kept spies out round about, to watch the movements of the Lamanites" (Alma 56:22), while also arranging for an additional two thousand men to be sent to them from Zarahemla. As the last of the additional men and provisions arrived, Helaman boldly declared, "And thus we were prepared with ten thousand men, and provisions for them, and also for their wives and their children" (Alma 56:28).

The stalemate continued with neither Nephites nor Lamanites wanting to leave their strongholds. The Lamanites, likely knowing of the provisions that had been delivered to Helaman in the city of Judea, grew fearful over the advantage that the added provisions and men were giving to the Nephite army. The Lamanites' fear that the Nephites were well supplied ultimately protected the Nephites and finally facilitated the defeat of the Lamanite army.

Do you remember the Nephite stratagem led by Antipus, who ordered Helaman to leave the safety of their well protected city of Judea to march with his sons toward a less prepared Nephite stronghold? Helaman reported that he was instructed to march with his sons "as if we were carrying provisions to a neighboring city. And it came to pass that we did march forth, as if with our provisions, to go to that city.

"And now, in the city Antiparah were stationed the strongest army of the Lamanites; yea, the most numerous. And it came to pass that when they had been informed by their spies, they came forth with their army and marched against us. And it came to pass that we did flee before them, northward. And thus we did lead away the most powerful army of the Lamanites" (Alma 56:30, 32, 34–36).

As the Lamanites left their stronghold in pursuit of Helaman and his band of men, a great chase ensued when the Nephite army led by Antipus began their pursuit of the Lamanites from behind. Caught between two great Nephite armies, the Lamanites were certainly filled with fear as they grew more and more desperate by the hour. Their only hope was to catch up to the stripling warriors to destroy them. Courageously, Helaman led his army farther north in a straight course and said, "Neither would I turn to the right nor to the left lest they should overtake me" (Alma 56:40). For three days, Helaman led this great chase with his well-prepared and certainly heavenly protected army, until finally the exhausted Lamanite army gave up the chase to regroup and reform their strategy.

Prepared with provisions and testimony, Helaman's army proceeded into battle fearing nothing and thus sustained the powerful words that would come to the prophet of the Restoration some two thousand years later: "If ye are prepared, ye shall not fear" (D&C 38:30).

Just as Helaman's army prepared to face great adversity, you too can pile on priesthood provisions to ensure that this period of preparation is equally provident for you and your modern band of stripling warriors. Greatest among the priesthood provisions that we can pursue is the preparation to know how to partake of the Atonement of Jesus Christ.

In following the example of Helaman to empower our sons with provisions before sending them into battle, we can look to another Father who prepared His children with priesthood power before sending them into this fallen world.

When Adam and Eve were first cast out of the Garden of Eden, their Heavenly Father surely felt a similar measure of compassion and a deep desire for them to return to Him someday. Leaning on the principles of the preparatory gospel, He empowered His first daughter and son with the necessary provisions to partake of Christ's Atonement and thus enabled their safe return to His presence. As Aaronic Priesthood holders partake of the Atonement, they will develop habits that are certain to fortify their testimony of Jesus Christ and develop a character that unifies them with the Master Himself. What greater priesthood provision can we provide our sons and daughters than the same provision that was given to Adam and Eve in their first days away from the garden? We are well served to teach our children how to partake of the Atonement in the same fashion that our Heavenly Father taught Adam and Eve:

> And he gave unto them commandments, that they should *worship the Lord their God,* and should *offer the firstlings of their flocks* . . . And *Adam was obedient* unto the Lord . . . This thing is *a similitude of the sacrifice of the Only Begotten* . . . *Thou shalt do all that thou doest in the name of the Son, and thou shalt repent, and call upon God in the name of the Son forevermore.* And *in that day* the Holy Ghost fell upon Adam. (Moses 5:5–9; emphasis added)

Shortly after being cast out of Eden, Adam and Eve began to encounter the realities of mortality and particularly the realities that come with parenting. At that time God introduced the Atonement of Jesus Christ and specifically taught them how to partake of its enabling, redeeming, and healing power. This message from our Heavenly Father to our first parents in the book of Moses contains the priesthood provisions for partaking of the Atonement that can unlock the eternal potential within each of us:

- Worship
- Offer
- Obey
- Consecrate (do all that thou doest in the name of the Son)
- Repent
- Endure to the end (call upon God forevermore)

It is worth pondering why the first commandment given to Adam and Eve was to worship the Lord their God and to consider what it means to worship. In His commandment for His children to worship, the Lord is seemingly looking to reaffirm His preeminent role in the universe as the creator of life upon whom we are all entirely dependent.

When we worship the Lord, we demonstrate our faith, in whatever state that may be, and in so doing we qualify ourselves to receive the Holy Ghost, through whom the tongues of angels can communicate the very personal and individual will of the Lord to each of us. Worshipping the Lord does not have to be complicated. His invitation is clear: "Draw near unto me and I will draw near unto you; seek me diligently and ye shall find me; ask, and ye shall receive; knock, and it shall be opened unto you . . . .Behold, that which you hear is as the voice of one crying in the wilderness—in the wilderness, because you cannot see him—my voice, because my voice is Spirit; my Spirit is truth; truth abideth and hath no end; and if it be in you it shall abound" (D&C 88:63).

We can draw unto Him in worship through prayer and meditation, studying the words and following the invitations of the prophets, and attending our church meetings. As we do this, His promise will be fulfilled and we shall hear His voice, even the voice of His Spirit, speaking truth that once received will be abundant within us.

How imperative this priesthood provision is for young Aaronic Priesthood holders. As Aaronic Priesthood holders understand the purpose of their worship, they can be inspired to honor this first commandment to worship the Lord their God and to qualify themselves for the loving and instructive whisper communicated by the Holy Ghost.

We see can see the powerful role that worship plays in partaking of the Atonement when we consider the simple example of a young man who is struggling to overcome a bad habit of swearing and using bad language. With a simple knowledge that swearing is an unbecoming habit, that young man will have the basic recognition of the need to create change and correct his language. He may have the thought to prepare himself for change with an effort to read his scriptures each night before bed. He may begin with a casual prayer that privately, but perhaps not yet entirely sincerely, acknowledges that he needs help to stop using bad language. With encouragement from parents and others who love him, this pattern of worship, still in its infancy, will have an impact as the Lord's promise is fulfilled: "And I will send upon him the Comforter, which shall teach him the truth and the way whither he shall go" (D&C 79:2).

It is among a parent's greatest duties to ensure that Aaronic Priesthood holders are empowered by the priesthood provision of worship. Specifically, families can help encourage personal and family worship by creating an environment conducive to discussing spiritual matters. We should have courage to bear our own sincere testimonies to one another in our families and to help each other discover our own sincerity in worship. As children wander, it is important for parents, siblings, and friends to be relatable, but we should not lose sight of our responsibility to elevate our conversations with our youth beyond what is just casual or contemporary. As we encourage them in their simple efforts to worship, we will help them in the individual quest that can only be theirs to learn the language of God's Holy Spirit, which language will enable them to partake of Christ's Atonement.

As holders of God's Aaronic Priesthood empowered with worship, valiant young men will come to better understand and fulfill their duty to both listen to and speak with the tongue of angels which will bless generations forever with this powerful priesthood provision of worshipping Almighty God.

In addition to commanding Adam and Eve to worship, the Lord commanded them to make offerings of the firstlings of their flocks, or to offer sacrifices unto Him. The order of events following Eden is instructive. First, Adam and Eve were asked to worship that they might qualify themselves for the soft whisperings of the Spirit. With the companionship of the Spirit, Adam and Eve could be instructed on what to change, or what they needed to give in order to receive the healing, enabling, and redeeming balm of the Atonement of Jesus Christ. The gospel plan for Adam and Eve was simple, just as it is for us today.

As holders of the Aaronic Priesthood are taught about sacrifice, they can discover for themselves the small changes, or sacrifices, that can help them draw unto the Savior. Only the Holy Ghost can communicate exactly what sacrifice a young man may need to make in his life. As a young man worships, the Lord invites him to "yield to the enticings of the Holy Spirit" (Mosiah 3:19). That young man may not be ready to yield, but at least he will begin to know what he must yield, give up, or simply what he must do to find true reconciliation with the Lord.

Let's return to our example of the young man overcoming his habit of swearing. As he begins to receive the fruits of his worship, he will certainly recognize specific things that he needs to do to facilitate the necessary change to draw closer to the Savior. He may feel prompted to change the music he listens to or perhaps the conversations that he participates in at school. Assuredly, at least some of these promptings will require him to give up something that may not be easy. He may even like a lot of the music with the explicit lyrics that he knows the Lord wants him to change. He may find it hard to give up the perceived popularity that he has achieved through his association with others at school who have similar habits.

Understandably, these changes will not be easy for a young man navigating his way through adolescence. It may take time for him to find it within himself to respond to these promptings.

God knew that repentance would not be easy for Adam, or any of his sons and daughters, so He provided the next invitation—to obey. In response to the Lord's invitations, Adam was obedient to the commandments of the Lord. Truly, Adam was an elect son of our Heavenly Father who quickly trusted the invitation of the Lord—even while he was still growing in his understanding of the Lord's purposes. This was most evident in his response to the angel who asked, "Why dost thou offer sacrifices unto the Lord?" Adam replied, "I know not, save the Lord commanded me" (Moses 5:6).

While some might immediately call attention to the example of Adam's unconditional, or even blind obedience, there is a deeper context to be gained when considering the more pervasive process of partaking of the Lord's Atonement.

Having prepared himself for the communications from the Holy Ghost through worship and having made initial efforts to obey the commandments and to make sacrifices, Adam was now in a position to receive pure personal revelation that would come as the angel taught him about the purpose of sacrifice: "This thing is a similitude of the Only Begotten of the Father which is full of grace and truth."

Again, as we apply Adam's obedience to ourselves, we begin to gain immense clarity into how practical the application of the Lord's Atonement can be for each of us. Let us return once again to the young man who recognized his need to overcome a problem with swearing.

Beginning with just the inkling of an acknowledgment of a problem, perhaps not even yet with a desire to change, the young man recognized a need for help. Because of his efforts to worship, he received guidance from the Holy Ghost about the sacrifices that would be required of him to facilitate change. Incumbent upon him now is the decision to exercise his agency to either obey or disobey the promptings that the Lord is sending specifically to him.

It is important to recognize that at first, this young man may not want to make those sacrifices. The Lord may have some requirements that do not make much sense to him because of his limited or obstructed view of himself and his problem. Like Adam, he may be called upon to have the courage to obey a prompting simply because he knows he "should" obey, rather than because he "desires" to obey. I think we can all relate to being in that state where we know what we "should" do, but it is not necessarily what we "want" to do, or even what we think is "fair."

Helaman's army stood as a sterling example in their obedience. Just as the Nephite army was on the brink of giving up to the immense pressure of the Lamanite armies, it was reported that "those two thousand and sixty were firm and undaunted. Yea, and they did obey and observe to perform every word of command with exactness; yea and even according to their faith it was done unto them and I [Moroni] did remember the words which they said unto me that their mothers had taught them" (Alma 57:21).

Like the sons of Helaman, you too will have need to find it within yourselves to be valiant, courageous, and even exact in your efforts to exercise your agency in obedience to the Lord's will. Your parents' primary purpose is to help you find the necessary courage and faith to partake of the Atonement. Empowered with an understanding of the priesthood provision of obedience, as modern-day stripling warriors, you will find strength to exercise your agency to act on the soft promptings of the Holy Ghost. As you respond in obedience, you will find that the motivations for your obedience will evolve and strengthen. You will move from a place of obedience out of obligation to a place of faith-based obedience where you are trusting that your efforts will be matched with power to overcome and to change who you are.

Finally, an equally important priesthood provision given to Adam came in the form of a commandment for Adam and Eve to consecrate themselves to the Lord: "Thou shalt do all that thou doest in the name of the Son" (Moses 5:8).

Here the Lord invokes a commandment for Adam to consecrate everything he does to Jesus Christ. This elevated invitation required Adam to more closely align his sacrifice to that of the Lord's by giving his whole self and all of his agency to the Savior.

Consider how this invitation might align with the preparatory gospel administered by the Aaronic Priesthood. In the sacrament prayer Aaronic Priesthood holders pray on behalf of those renewing their covenants and promise the Lord that those who partake of the sacred emblems will always remember Him. In this simple statement, covenant members of Christ's preparatory gospel can relate to the commandment given to Adam. In effect, it would be impossible for one who is always remembering Him to do anything without it being done in the name of Jesus Christ.

Through the preparatory elements of the sacrament and the concept of "always remembering," we can gain a simplified understanding of the doctrine of consecration. Through both logic and faith, those who sincerely seek to understand the Lord's will and to be obedient through sacrifice will inevitably develop a desire to follow the Savior's admonition to the Nephites: "For the works that ye have seen me do that shall ye also do" (3 Nephi 27:21).

Ultimately as we work to sacrifice, obey, and consecrate ourselves we will convey our newfound love of the Lord by seeking to always remember Him in every thought, word, and action. In so doing we will find that we are coming to know Him and are prepared to be changed through His Atonement to become like Him.

With the provisions of worship, sacrifice, and obedience in his quiver, Adam was soon further commanded by the angel: "Wherefore, thou shalt do all that thou doest in the name of the Son, and thou shalt repent and call upon God in the name of the Son forevermore" (Moses 5:8).

I love the language that points us to understanding and conforming to the will of the Lord. The doctrine taught to Adam pointed him to a process that would allow him to experience real change as he became a saint, having washed himself in the blood of the Lamb to become not only aligned, but ultimately unified, with Christ.

Our young man overcoming a problem with the simple challenge of using inappropriate language can pursue this unity with Christ as he follows the pattern outlined to Adam. Starting with a basic acknowledgment of the separation from the Lord that his actions have created, he has worshipped to qualify himself for instruction that has led to an understanding of a sacrifice that he must make, requiring courage, faith, and obedience to exercise the agency required to give his offering to the Lord. In so doing, he participates in an expiatory process that follows the infinite model established by the Savior Himself.

Like any father, I remember when my son was just a young boy. I would occasionally find him stumbling out of my closet with a huge smile on his face and my size 11 shoes on his tiny, and wrong, feet. In this endearing episode that occurs in just about every household, a simple but important principle can be observed. For a boy to become like his father, he must do the things that his father does. He must be willing to stumble in those uncomfortable and oversized shoes. To become like his father, the boy must come to truly know his father and his mannerisms. Certainly, in time, that boy will grow and become like his father.

The process of becoming like the Savior is identical. For a boy to become like the Savior, he must fumble in the closet to find the shoes. He must spend time with the Lord to come to know His ways and His voice. Ultimately, he must walk as He walks, even taking upon himself the yoke of the Master.

Think for a moment of how the process taught to Adam demonstrates the example set by Jesus that allows all of His sons and daughters to truly become like Him. Like Jesus, Adam too recognized that he had an important need to draw all men unto Him. Like Jesus, Adam worshipped through prayer to draw on Heavenly help. Like Jesus, Adam received spiritual direction regarding the infinite sacrifice that would be required of him. Like Jesus, as Adam exercised his agency, he ensured that his will was perfectly aligned with his Father. In so doing, Adam experienced a conversion of his own in which, by following the example of the Savior of the world, like Jesus, he was eternally unified with God.

In the most intimate and sacred way possible, Adam set the example for all of God's children to become just like Jesus as they repent. Like Adam, we can worship and receive revelation, exercise agency to be obedient, and offer sacrifice. As we do this, we will experience that great change of heart spoken of by prophets in which our desire to follow the will of the Lord will evolve from obligation with minimal understanding of purpose to motivation by true love and gratitude for the Savior and the salvation granted through His eternal sacrifice. We will develop a desire to follow the angel's invitation to Adam to commit to a life pursuing this process of change that we call repentance by "calling upon God forevermore."

By empowering yourself with not only understanding but also daily experiences with these priesthood provisions, you will align and ultimately unify your agency with the will of the Lord.

The process of aligning our will through this process of partaking of the Atonement of Jesus Christ is a lifelong endeavor. It is foolish to think that this powerful process can be simplified to an easy-to-follow recipe with perfectly predictable outcomes. However, what can be counted on is that with each effort to close the gap between ourselves and God, we will find a beautiful experience in which we will gain an increased understanding of the perfect nature of Jesus Christ. As you pursue this process, you can be assured that the Lord's promises are perfectly available to you to become sanctified and prepared for a joy-filled life on the covenant path.

As Adam learned and accepted each invitation to partake of the atonement, he received a blessing and a promise: "And in that day the Holy Ghost fell upon Adam, which beareth record of the Father and the Son, saying: I am the Only Begotten of the Father from the beginning, henceforth and forever, *that as thou has fallen thou mayest be redeemed, and all mankind, even as many as will*" (Moses 5:9; emphasis added).

Adam's blessing is your blessing and mine. As we partake of the Atonement of Jesus Christ, we will receive the Holy Ghost, who will bear witness of the Father and the Son. As you and I fall, and we all do, redemption will be available to each of us. By partaking of the Atonement, Aaronic Priesthood holders will come to know in a very personal way of this sacred promise from the Lord: "Therefore, sanctify yourselves that your minds become single to God, *and the days will come that you shall see him*; for the will unveil his face unto you, and it shall be in his own time, and in his own way, and according to his own will" (D&C 88:68; emphasis added).

I love the fact that the word "days" is plural in this verse. While the verse certainly promises of days beyond this life when the Lord shall show His face, I like to think that as children of God sanctify themselves and bring their minds into singularity or unity with God, there may be many days in which we "see" the face of the Lord in small but poignant ways. Your parents and leaders can be confident that the days will come when they will see the face of the Lord in you, the Aaronic Priesthood holders they love, as they report on their stewardship of you, just as Helaman accounted for his sons: "Now this was the faith of these of whom I have spoken; they are young, and their minds are firm, and they do put their trust in God" (Helaman 57:27).

By partaking of the Atonement, we all can come to know the Master we have served and will have an increased capacity to recognize Him when we see His presence in our lives. It is my experience that we will be given opportunities to "see" Him as we utilize these powerful priesthood provisions to partake of His Atonement and consecrate our thoughts, actions, and even our whole selves to Him who is mighty to save.

A Pattern of Courage to Create Confidence

Never had I seen so great courage.

After three days of leading the Lamanites away from their stronghold city of Antiparah, Helaman's band certainly would have been weary. When the light of that third morning came, they saw the Lamanites upon them again, and once again they began to march, not turning to the right or the left, leading the Lamanites deep into the wilderness. However, after just a short distance on this third morning, the Lamanites suddenly gave up their pursuit.

Helaman's army did not know if their enemies had been caught by Antipus or if they had stopped to set a trap to draw the young army to return to them. In his unending wisdom, Helaman trusted in his now well-prepared band of brothers to evaluate and decide for themselves how their mission should now conclude by inviting the young soldiers to dictate their own destiny, asking them, "Therefore what say ye, my sons, will ye go against them to battle?" (Alma 56:44).

Well-prepared from a life of obedience and faith, having been nurtured by their mothers, and with the liberty of their fathers at the forefront of their minds, Helaman's sons replied without hesitation: "Father, behold our God is with us, and he will not suffer that we should fall" (Alma 56:46).

With great pride, Helaman wrote to Moroni of their bravery: "Never had I seen so great courage, nay, not amongst all the Nephites" (Alma 56:45).

Helaman's army embodied the dictionary definition of courage as defined by Merriam-Webster in possessing the "mental or moral strength to venture, persevere, and withstand danger, fear, or difficulty."[1] Empowered with priesthood and prepared by experience, Helaman's soldiers individually responded to the call to battle without hesitation. They had done hard things before and were supremely confident in the source of their protection. Filled with faith, they did not fear.

In contemplating their courage, I find it insightful to consider this observation by Helaman: "Now they never had fought, yet they did not fear death" (Alma 56:47). It is easy to overlook that after reading for nearly an entire chapter about these young soldiers, we are reminded of this small detail, that after all that we have read about Helaman's army, they still had yet to lift their swords.

Remember all of the things that had transpired before their first actual call to battle: These brave young soldiers had never before engaged in combat. They had volunteered to step forward in place of their parents, only because their parents had covenanted to not take up weapons against the Lamanites. Even still, Helaman would not lead them into battle until *after* they had marched to the city of Judea to assist and strengthen the army of Antipus; until *after* they had been prepared and preserved by the hand of the Lord who had stayed the Lamanite army from attacking them in their time of weakness; until *after* they had spent at least several months fortifying themselves and their defenses of the city; until *after* a disappointing failed stratagem to draw the Lamanites out of their stronghold; until *after* waiting what was possibly nearly an entire year to receive additional provisions from their fathers; and finally, not until *after* they had fully exhausted themselves following three days of fleeing the bloodthirsty Lamanites. In his wisdom, Helaman saw the need to ensure that a patient preparation was complete before calling on his young soldiers to engage in battle with the Lamanites.

Despite never having actually fought, these young but well-prepared soldiers were confident because of all that had transpired in preparation for this heroic moment. Helaman notes some of the underlying elements that enabled such courage: "They did think more upon the liberty of their fathers than they did upon their lives; yea, they had been taught by their mothers, that if they did not doubt, God would deliver them" (Alma 56:47).

Sustaining their courage was their sense of purpose and their unwavering confidence in their God. Leaning on their preparatory experiences, they were well equipped to answer the call. It is also important to recognize that at the time of Helaman's invitation to go into battle, the young army was not compelled by their captain or anyone else, but rather they retained their complete agency to choose to honor their parents, their liberty, and their God to turn about face to pursue and to fight the Lamanites. Certainly they could have accepted a more cowardly lot by celebrating their escape without questioning why the Lamanites had suddenly given up the chase. Instead they responded in faith, turning their march around with the ferocity of lions to conquer the enemy of their peace.

You know the rest of the story. These brave stripling warriors soon fell upon the Lamanites, who were on the brink of conquering the Nephites, having already killed their brave captain, Antipus. So great was Helaman's onslaught that the entire Lamanite army turned away from the army of Antipus to defend themselves, and in the end Helaman proclaimed: "But behold, to my great joy, there had not one soul of them fallen to the earth; yea, and they had fought as if with the strength of God; yea, never were men known to have fought with such miraculous strength; and with such mighty power did they fall upon the Lamanites, that they did frighten them; and for this cause did the Lamanites deliver themselves up as prisoners of war" (Alma 56:56).

In acknowledging the bravery of Helaman's army, it is important to recognize that they were not emboldened with this courage overnight. Rather, it manifested itself only after many weeks, months, and even years of preparation in which they had been guided and mentored by their parents, more senior Nephite soldiers, and their captain. Key to their preparation was being challenged to lift heavy burdens while the consequences of failure were still relatively light.

We saw an example of that preparation in that first march to support and comfort the beleaguered army of Antipus at Judea.

Helaman's wisdom to lead them in a less risky but appropriately challenging mission proved instrumental in instilling the confidence necessary to respond without hesitation to the call of their captain. Ultimately, this confidence enabled them to deliver the results that would protect and preserve the liberty of their loved ones later on when the consequences meant everything.

Like Helaman, you Aaronic Priesthood holders will undoubtedly one day be called into battles where the stakes are high, when you will be playing for absolute keeps. For many, some of your first calls for real courage may be to overcome the eviscerating temptations of mortality. It may also be in the form of facing the wonderful but often overwhelming call to missionary service. Other calls for bravery will come when educational pursuits are on the line and difficult priorities must be managed with absolute discipline. Certainly faith, confidence, and courage will be requisite when you kneel together at an altar with an equally courageous young woman and together enter on the high and holy covenant path.

With these important calls for courage and confidence in mind, the six fleeting years as Aaronic Priesthood holders take on even greater significance as the critical season of preparation that they are. Because of this, parents and leaders are inherently charged with an often-daunting responsibility to ensure that within their respective stewardship, these formative years do not slip away without proper preparation. It is our solemn responsibility as parents and leaders to not leave you Aaronic Priesthood holders fettered by our failures. Instead, it is our charge to help you find opportunities to develop courage and confidence when consequences are low.

As Aaronic Priesthood leaders erect and ultimately remove the scaffolding that will build boys into the priesthood men that the Lord needs in his army, they must recognize the power that comes with purposeful preparation. Throughout these chapters, we have contemplated many examples of purposeful preparation. As you review some of these in your mind, consider how each example required each young man to be challenged, to lift a burden that was heavy—to him, to simply do something that he might have deemed as difficult. Contemplate how by being challenged, these young men would have been just a little more prepared for a day when real courage would be required to respond to a call to step onto a real battlefield with confidence in their abilities and in their God to come off conqueror.

Remember the deacons who were challenged for courage to prepare a spiritual thought as they added their stick to the campfire that they surrounded together with their peers.

Remember the teacher who was challenged by the bishop to exercise courage in ministering to the needs of the single mother by organizing a service project to get her yard ready for summer.

Remember the priests who were increased in confidence and faith in their purposeful assignment to minister to members of the ward as they courageously overcame their anxiety by preparing and delivering *Preach My Gospel* missionary messages within the safety of their ward.

Purposeful preparation to challenge young men to develop courage and confidence should permeate every assignment and activity, whether simple or elaborate. I once felt greatly inspired by the purposeful preparation and vision of one teachers quorum who identified an opportunity to challenge themselves in the form of a summer activity. As you read the account of this quorum activity, pay attention to the ways in which the advisers followed the example of Helaman to identify purpose in their planning as they challenged the courage of a group of fourteen- and fifteen–year-olds and delivered on their assignment to facilitate a true preparatory experience that is certain to be foundational in the lives of these powerful priesthood holders.

Here is the account of their summer camping activity as reported in the *Provo Daily Herald* on June 17, 2016:

> Lake Powell is a popular summer destination for many Utahns, but not many people travel there the way one Lehi Scout troop did a few weeks ago.
>
> When Ryan Kirby and Lothar Alomia, co-leaders of the Eagle Crest Third Ward Varsity Scout crew 1080 of The Church of Jesus Christ of Latter-day Saints, sat down with their seven 14– and 15–year-olds in January to plan the summer's high adventure camp experience,

they had no idea that their group would end up biking 206.5 miles from Lehi to Lake Powell.

"The boys said they wanted to go to Lake Powell, and I think my response was, 'That's a vacation, not high adventure.' So I facetiously told them, 'Okay, but you have to ride your bikes there,'" Kirby said.

The boys took the idea seriously, though.

"We didn't actually think it would be as hard as it was," said Aidan Merrell, 15.

"It's kinda one of those things that seems like a good idea, and then you actually do it," Bridger Pack, 15, laughed.

From February through May, the crew prepped with a spinning class and regular bike rides every week. Boys being boys, they didn't take the training seriously, and every one of them wished they had.

On May 30, with a big neighborhood send-off, the seven boys, two leaders and a few other support crew fathers rode away from their LDS church building in east Lehi. Using mostly borrowed $1,000 road bikes, that first day they biked 72 miles—from Lehi, through Goshen Canyon, to Levan. They camped in Torrey for the night.

There were a lot of elevation gains throughout that day, and it was a tough day of pedaling. But their peloton was protected in front by their water truck, and in back by their supply truck. The rear truck was adorned with a sign declaring their ride, and that got them a lot of shouts of encouragement from passing drivers and motorcyclists.

"We got a lot of love," Aidan said.

The mileage of the trip's second day was less—about 65 miles, with a lot of downhill stretches—but it was a tough one. The troop got a later start, and after the highlight of passing through Capitol Reef National Park, with its picturesque vistas and views, the group struggled with heat, crashes and some tough hills.

"Everything was going great until we left the park [Capitol Reef]. We hit some 6 and 8 percent climbs, and it was hot. That's the most god-forsaken country in the state of Utah," Kirby said. "Fatigue set in, the scenery was desolate. It made it a hard afternoon."

Stuart Loper, 14, crashed when his bike chain slipped off as the group headed out after Capitol Reef. He rode in the truck for part of the day, but soon got back out on the bike, so he wouldn't miss out on getting his biking mileage in.

On the third day, they still had at least 60 more miles from Hanksville to Lake Powell. They learned from their day two mistake, and headed out as early as they could to beat the heat as much as possible. The first 30 miles weren't too bad, but then they hit what they nicknamed, "Hell's Hills," after the turn off towards Bullfrog Basin Marina.

"You'd go up, then slightly downhill, then up again. It was climb after climb," said Christian Johnson, 14.

Though the terrain was uphill, things started going downhill. Zack Bowers, 14, got heat exhaustion, and though he tried to get back out on the bike after a short stint cooling down, he was forced to stay in the truck most of the rest of the day. Soon after, Dane Kargis, 15, hit Aidan's back wheel and flew off his bike, thrashing both knees. Bridger, who was close behind him, knocked into Dane's head as he tried to get out of the way.

"When we got home, we all had these welcome banners on our garages, and his mom wrote on my sign, 'Thanks for running over my son,'" Bridger laughed.

Still, these boys were so determined to get in as much of their full 200 miles as possible, so after a small rest, and some major bandaging, Dane, too, was back on his bike. Finally, the whole crew rode—sweaty, bloodied, but triumphantly—straight down to the water's edge at Lake Powell around 3 p.m. that day. They camped at Lake Powell for the next three days, swimming, tubing, wakeboarding, cliff-jumping and hiking.

While the lake was fun, the journey allowed them to become close as a group, and learn some solid lifelong lessons.

"I learned how amazingly awesome these people are," said Budge Hyde, 15, of the boys and leaders. "I had some major anxiety and sickness out there, but they got me through it."

"We're all parts of a body, in a way, and each part is important. When one person is doing good, we all did good. When one fell behind, we all fell behind," Christian said.

They all also were a bit surprised at what they actually achieved, and a few of them are interested in doing another 100–mile bike ride.

"You can do hard things. If you practice and try, you can do things you didn't think you could," Bridger said.[2]

I love the statements of courage made by these young men. Read some of them again with me and contemplate the impact that this activity had on their priesthood preparation and the development of their own courage and confidence:

- "We didn't actually think it would be as hard as it was."

- "It's kinda one of those things that seems like a good idea, and then you actually do it."
- "We got a lot of love."
- "You'd go up, then slightly downhill, then up again. It was climb after climb."
- "When we got home, we all had these welcome banners."
- "I learned how amazingly awesome these people are. I had some major anxiety and sickness out there, but they got me through it."
- "We're all parts of a body in a way, and each part is important. When one person is doing good, we all did good. When one fell behind, we all fell behind."
- "You can do hard things. If you practice and try, you can do things you didn't think you could."

I love how the story barely mentions the fun these boys had at Lake Powell. Certainly, the reward for their efforts was fantastic, but the impact was in accomplishing something that was hard, something that required real work and consistent effort. These advisers were not compelled to provide an entertaining vacation. Instead they capitalized on an idea that started as a facetious remark. They recognized the immense value in challenging boys to do hard things.

When planning is purposeful, these preparatory years as Aaronic Priesthood holders can be powerful. The confidence of these young men was increased immeasurably as they were challenged in a very difficult task while still protected by relatively low consequences for failure.

Like the army of Helaman inspired by their own preparatory successes, these young men are now far better equipped to manage the emotional rigors of missionary service and marriage.

Undoubtedly, proud parents and leaders were given ample opportunities to see how each boy responded when faced with challenging circumstances. Astute as they certainly were, in this experience, these parents likely identified certain unique needs within each young man that required continued individual ministry as their Aaronic Priesthood holder continued in his priesthood preparation. Courage is a requirement in a daunting world. In raising a royal army, our soldiers must discover for themselves this Christ-like attribute and there is no better place than within the constructs of Aaronic Priesthood service.

In the words of President Thomas S. Monson, "Courage counts." In the October 1986 general conference, President Monson said:

> Of course, we will face fear, experience ridicule, and meet opposition. Let us have the courage to defy the consensus, the courage to stand for principle. Courage, not compromise, brings the smile of God's approval. Courage becomes a living and an attractive virtue when it is regarded not only as a willingness to die manfully, but as the determination to live decently. A moral coward is one who is afraid to do what he thinks is right because others will disapprove or laugh. Remember that all men have their fears, but those who face their fears with dignity have courage as well.
>
> My brethren let us be active participants—not mere spectators—on the stage of priesthood power. May we muster courage at the crossroads, courage for the conflicts, courage to say no, courage to say yes, for courage counts.[3]

Courage not only counts, but it is crucial in developing the confidence of powerful priesthood holders. When parents and advisers seek the perspective of Helaman, they are blessed with the vision to see each of their young soldiers, awkward as they may be in their oversized armor, as powerful, well-prepared men of God. With this vision of who you, as an Aaronic Priesthood holder, can become, you will find promised success in priesthood service that will challenge your courage and construct your confidence as a humble holder of the royal priesthood of God.

NOTES

1. Merriam-Webster's online dictionary. See merriam-webster.com/dictionary/courage?utm_campaign=sd&utm_medium=serp&utm_source=jsonld. Accessed May 22, 2020.
2. Karissa Neely, "LDS teen group bikes from Lehi to Lake Powell in 3 days," *Provo Daily Herald*, June 17, 2016. See heraldextra.com/news/local/north/lehi/lds-teen-group-bikes-from-lehi-to-lake-powell-in

article_05a6ae63–c04b-51a9–9a2d-3f2a32b0d0b1.html. Accessed May 22, 2020. Used by permission of the author.

3. Thomas S. Monson, "Courage Counts," churchofjesuschrist.org/study/general-conference/1986/10/courage-counts?lang=eng. Accessed May 26, 2020.

CONCLUSION

The Lord needs a powerful priesthood. He truly does have a work for you to do. He needs you, whoever you are, to do your part to harness the power of the Aaronic Priesthood. The clear purpose of this priesthood is to prepare people for the coming of the Lord. He will come. There is no room for doubt. We are living in the winding-up scenes of this great and last dispensation. The Lord needs priesthood holders now who can stand at the door and hold it open, extending to all of the chosen vessels that glorious invitation to come unto Christ. Only an Aaronic Priesthood holder can hold the door open for all of God's children to receive His covenant.

The temple baptistry now allows holders of the Aaronic Priesthood to fulfill their priesthood duty to extend their sacred invitation to come unto Christ. I love seeing a young priest standing in the water of the temple baptistry with his arm reverently raised. I have been particularly touched when sitting quietly and listening to a young priest repeat over and over the words, "Having been commissioned of Jesus Christ . . ."

What better commission could there be than to be called, authorized, and commanded to conduct this simple ordinance of opening the door to the kingdom of God on behalf of the Savior? Being commissioned of Jesus Christ is to be a fellow servant with John the Baptist and millions of other worthy and dedicated Aaronic Priesthood holders and sustaining sisters. Like them, you have been commissioned to fulfill the purposes of the Aaronic Priesthood as you do your duty and act in the name of the Messiah. May you be blessed wherever you are and in whatever capacity you have to accept this commission and sustain the power of the Aaronic Priesthood as you claim your priesthood privilege to prepare a people for the coming of the Lord.

ABOUT THE AUTHOR

Nathan K. Nelson has a passion for seeing scriptures beneath their surface and using them to mentor Aaronic Priesthood holders. His unique ability to lay low so that others may grow has earned respect from those he has served. Prior to writing *Upon You My Fellow Servants*, he authored only obnoxious text messages to his patient wife, Kara, and sentimental Christmas letters to his three amazing daughters and one-of-a-kind son.

When not planning the next family vacation or loading skis onto the family car, you can find Nathan traveling in a Delta window seat organizing his thoughts for his next soapbox sermon. Nathan holds a bachelor of arts degree from the University of Utah and a master of business administration degree from Brigham Young University.